Unusual Motorcycles

A collection of curious concepts, prototypes and race bikes

Acknowledgements

The list is long, as research into the rare, the unsaid and the unusual requires many documents to be consulted and much assistance to be solicited.

My thanks first of all to *La Vie de la Moto* magazine, the weekly rendezvous for all French vintage motorbike enthusiasts, which originally published these articles; to its director, Alain Georges, who gave the go-ahead for this project and to its editor-in-chief, Philippe Bidaut, who week after week has enthusiastically supported my column.

Particular thanks go to Yves Campion, the outstanding Belgian collector and specialist on Gillet motorbikes, who did the title-page drawings for each chapter, and who opened his files to me. Thank you also to Pierre Ducloux and Jean Bourdache whose writings on the early days of the motorcycle have brought me much enlightenment. Thanks to all the photographers whose precious work illustrates this book. Thank you also to the often-anonymous authors, whose writings have provided the material for these pages. Thank you to my wife Lana, who read the text and helped me to choose the most relevant material in the face of limited space! My thanks finally to you, the reader, for the interest you have shown in these unusual motorbikes. It is your curiosity that makes history come alive.

First published in the French language as 'Motos insolites & prototypes hors normes' in June 2011 by E-T-A-I. This English-language edition published by Haynes in October 2012.

A catalogue record for this book is available from the British Library

ISBN 978 0 85733 261 5

Library of Congress control card no 2012938593

Published by Haynes Publishing,
Sparkford, Yeovil, Somerset BA22 7JJ, UK
Tel: 01963 442030 Fax: 01963 440001
Int. tel: +44 1963 442030 Int. fax: +44 1963 440001
E-mail: sales@haynes.co.uk
Website: www.haynes.co.uk

Translated by Ken Smith

Haynes North America Inc.,
861 Lawrence Drive, Newbury Park, California 91320, USA

Printed and bound in the USA by Odcombe Press LP,
1299 Bridgestone Parkway, La Vergne, TN 37086

Photographic credits

Any uncredited photos and illustrations generally belong to the author, who apologises in advance if any sources have been overlooked.

Every effort has been made to locate copyright holders. We apologise for any unintended errors or omissions, which we would be happy to correct in any future edition. We hope that this edition may reveal the names of any copyright holders, to whom we extend the usual rights.

Graphic design: Sophie Pujols

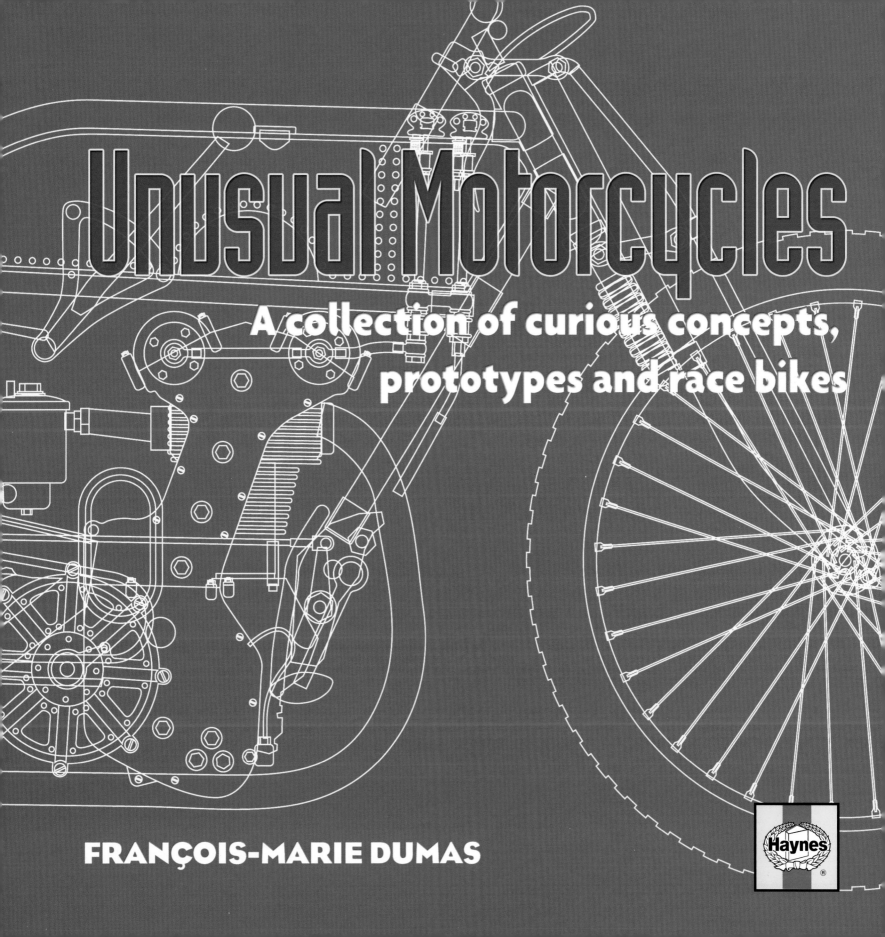

Unusual Motorcycles

A collection of curious concepts, prototypes and race bikes

FRANÇOIS-MARIE DUMAS

Haynes

DEAR READER,

For some years now, I have contributed a few pages to the French magazine *La Vie de la Moto (LVM)*, devoted to the history of the motorcycle, but with an emphasis on oddities and little secrets, on those unusual, out-of-the-ordinary bikes, the original, the weird, the zany, the preposterous, the incredible and all those that, often unfortunately for them, were ahead of their time.

The very nature of this large-format weekly, principally devoted to the topic of vintage motorcycles, makes filing difficult. With this in mind, we present this anthology of the 'pages of history' that were published in *LVM*, often with the addition of new photos and other details. We make no claim to be encyclopaedic or exhaustive in the compilation, which is divided into six broad categories arranged in chronological order.

Happy reading!

FRANÇOIS-MARIE DUMAS
2012

CONTENTS

RACING MOTORCYCLES

MOTORCYCLES AND SIDECARS

SCOOTERS

UNUSUAL
MOTORCYCLES

600cc Killinger & Freund three-cylinder two-stroke,
Germany 1938. (Drawing by Yves Campion)

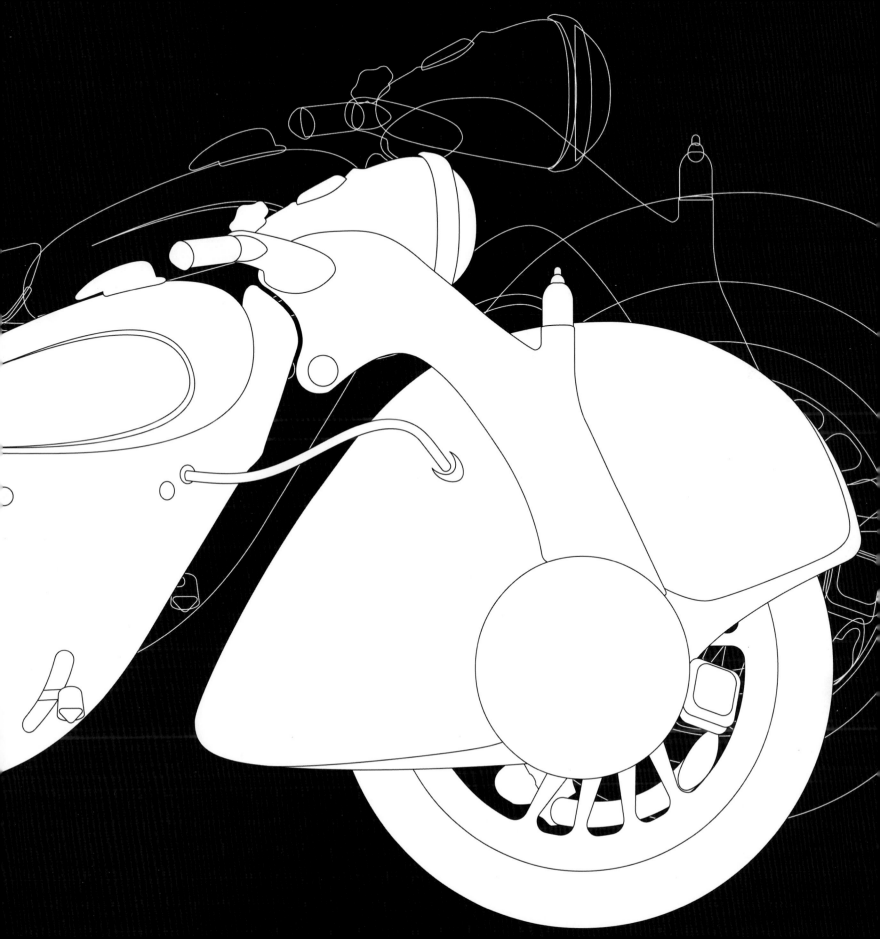

FÉLIX MILLET (1895—1897)
The first multi-cylinder motorcycle at the age of 120

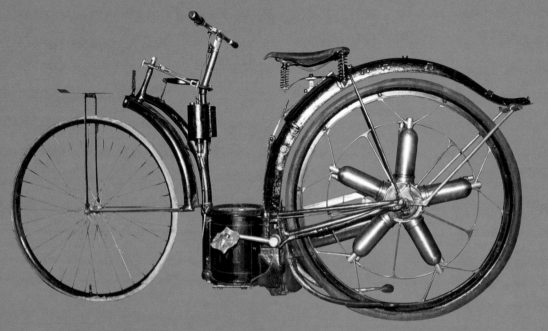

An amazing early forerunner packed with innovations: radial, multi-cylinder engine, front and rear swingarm suspension and lots more. Let's take a look...

In 1887, 16 years after Louis-Guillaume Perreaux's steam bike, the first powered two-wheeler aimed at the market, and two years after Gottlieb Daimler had put an internal combustion engine on to a rudimentary wooden frame with two cartwheels and a pair of laterally mounted stabilisers, the inspired Félix Millet built his 'sun wheel' with its five cylinders mounted radially, and an embryonic suspension system with the engine mounted on 15 spring-like, flexible rings! The following year, he used it as the front wheel of a tricycle and patented it in late 1888, making him the officially recognised inventor of the rotating radial engine (the drive shaft was fixed and the engine turned with the wheel), not to be confused with the fixed radial engine. In those enlightened days, you built something first and patented it afterwards.

The future lies in motorised bikes

Félix was convinced that the future lay in motorised two-wheelers and he devoted himself to them. But the competition was tough. Paul Daimler, Gottlieb's son, covered 3km in his father's 'motorised wheelbarrow' on 10 November 1885, and the Hildebrand & Wolfmüller, patented in 1894, first turned a wheel in June of the same year. Millet's first petroleum-fuelled bicycle, of 1894, with its five-cylinder radial engine on the rear wheel, created a sensation at the Second Cycle Show organised in December 1894 by the Paris Employers' Federation. This pioneering show brought together 350 exhibitors and on display for the first time were a De Dion Bouton steam tricycle and two motorcycles: the Pétrolette, presented by Duncan & Superbie — actually a German Hildebrand & Wolfmüller 'Frenchified' for the occasion — and, on the Gladiator Cycles stand, the remarkable Félix Millet. His sun wheel had evolved, abandoning the suspension of the engine within the wheel, as Millet had designed a front suspension with a leading-link fork relying on the flex in the horizontal arms supporting the wheel and resting via a saddle on a leaf spring that formed the mudguard! The offset steering worked using a system of rods and the crank gear chain was encased. There's nothing better than some competition to test the worth of a product and,

Spider-like, in this 1895 version, the Millet with its 1,925cm 'sun wheel' has an output of 1.2hp at 180rpm and a maximum rpm of 325. It weighs 60kg, of which the engine contributes just 10kg, while the induction coil weighs 4kg and the battery 8kg. The battery acid needed changing almost as often as the fuel tank needed filling! The front suspension, the first of its kind, was the leading link type with two flexible, spring-steel arms carrying the wheel and an upper leaf spring acting as a shock absorber. (Musée des Arts et Métiers, Paris)

A photo of the first test ride, annotated by Félix Millet himself. The back-to-back tricycle dates from 1869 and the front 'sun wheel' was made in 1887. Notice the engine suspension by spring rings and the lack of any tyres. (Lycée Technique Hippolyte-Fontaine Collection, Dijon)

What a tangled web on this 1896 Millet! All the parts are inside so their operation is quite hard to follow. Parts of the riveted metal frame act as a mudguard, air-inlet manifold and fuel tank! The large, white, porcelain hub ahead of the crank gear is the ignition battery (a Millet patent), which operates after half a turn to mix the constituent acids (nitric and sulphuric). The front suspension is similar to that on the 1895 Millet, and the same principle is used at the rear, with a swingarm pivoting on the crank gear axis. The arm bears on an arched bar guided by two rods and attached to the mudguard by a shock-absorbing extension spring. The two left-hand tubes serve as a casing for the chain. The middle tube on this side acts both as the exhaust pipe and a torsion bar for the suspension! (Lycée Technique Hippolyte-Fontaine Collection, Dijon)

Air taken in below the front of the saddle (adjustable with a slider) is heated by the exhaust gases fed through the middle tube/torsion bar near the crank gear. It then passes through the upper right-hand tube of the swing arm to be mixed with petrol and vaporised through the inlet valves. Finally, in the centre of the wheel, you can see the lubrication feed, although we'll let you work out where the circuit goes... it's all inside, of course!
(Lycée Technique Hippolyte-Fontaine Collection, Dijon)

usefully, a certain Marquis de Dion organised the first big international race on 11 June 1895, from Paris to Bordeaux and back: 1,200km to be covered in one go in less than 100 hours. The Félix Millet, which had made its first public outing in the spring, confidently took its place on the start line. None of the two- or three-wheelers finished, but the Millet managed to cover 54km in three hours eight minutes before dropping out.

Unsuccessful production

Happy with the outcome, Félix Millet decide to market it and got Alexandre Darracq (the builder of Gladiator cycles) to construct a second 'production' version, which appeared in 1897 and is illustrated on this and the following pages.

This extraordinary machine was packed with innovations: a radial engine, battery-coil ignition and contact breaker, automatic-mixer lubrication, handlebars that when swivelled forward automatically lowered a double kickstand, a clutch operated by the handgrip or by backpedalling and a link to the brake. Still more impressive, the rear part of the hollow frame served as the fuel tank and mudguard; swing suspension was fitted both front and rear; the transmission chain from the pedal crank (used in starting and for extra power) ran inside the tubes of the rear swingarm... What an engineer! The whole thing weighed 60kg and was clocked at 53km/h in 1898.

It was too clever by half and ahead of its time. Simply too good, in fact, for only one or two examples of this remarkable machine were produced at the Suresnes factory. The down-to-earth Alexandre Darracq, realising that a straightforward, single-cylinder model like the Werner or the de Dion had more of a future than a five-cylinder radial, abandoned the project.

Yet many of the technical features pioneered on the Millet would be used successfully in the subsequent decades; it was just too much, too soon.

Furthermore, the Millet would have a noble lineage, with the Seguin brothers, founders of Gnome & Rhône (now Snecma), taking over and developing the five-cylinder, radial, rotary engine idea and using it in 1907 in their first product, the Omega, a seven-cylinder, radial, rotary aero engine.

Another on the way!

Such a jewel in France's mechanical heritage had to be safeguarded and the Lycée Technique Hippolyte-Fontaine in Dijon, which has looked after the second version of the Félix Millet in its original state, recently decided to give it a second life. The machine has been very carefully dismantled, its parts measured and redrawn so that an exact replica can be constructed for exhibition. When can we have a ride? My name is on the waiting list!

Brilliant! Raising the handlebars pulls a cable that lowers the two kickstands. Two handles work, respectively, the throttle and the clutch. Below the handlebars, to the left, is the HT ignition coil; to the right is a close-up of the ancestor of the separate lubrication of modern two-strokes, with a tank containing three different sorts of oil for the 'automatic' lubricator, metered by valves at the outlets. (Lycée Technique Hippolyte-Fontaine Collection, Dijon)

This photo of the first version gives a good view of the remote steering system, the enclosed crank-gear transmission chain, the rear mudguard with its built-in fuel tank, and the kickstands (controlled by a lever under the saddle) that hinge out to the side. (Musée des Arts et Métiers, Paris)

A noted engineer attempts to fathom the arcane workings of the Millet.

Moto Félix Millet

Michel Pernot,
secrétaire du Club des Motocyclettistes
donnera une conférence
sur

Félix Millet
sa vie et ses motos

Jeudi 14 février de 16 à 17 heures

● ● ● ● Five-cylinder, four-stroke, radial engine that rotates with the wheel; air cooled – 1,924cc (70 x 100mm) – 1.2hp at 366rpm – Distribution by two valves operated by tappets in a tube on the outside of the cylinder, one being the inlet tract (right side) and the other the exhaust (left side) to the central hub – Battery-coil HT ignition – Surface carburettor – Semi-automatic lubrication mixing – Clutch engagement by backpedalling (with the brake) or rotating handle – Pedal starting – Open frame from tubes and riveted sheet – Leading-link front suspension, rear swing – Approx. 60kg (engine 10kg) – 55km/h (34mph).

LOUIS CLÉMENT (1920—1921)
The exception

f we were obliged to retain only the 10 or so most interesting examples from the history of motorcycles, the Louis Clément would be worthy of its place among them. Following in Louis Blériot's footsteps, this French aviation pioneer turned to the motorcycle after the war, producing this masterpiece in 1919.

Specialists in making metal parts, particularly for the aeronautical industry, the Louis Clément Company (no connection with Adolphe Clément and his equally well-known motorbikes), with factories at Lyon, Bordeaux and Boulogne-Billancourt, put all their experience and tooling capacity into the production, at the last-named works, of this unusual machine, which first appeared in 1919 and was sold, in small numbers, from 1920 until late 1921.

An overhead camshaft and a single head for two cylinders

At a time when the most rudimentary engineering was the norm, the Louis Clément offered a two-cylinder V-engine with a single overhead camshaft driven by bevel gears and a shaft. The use of a single cylinder head and OHC for the two V cylinders was unique and caused such oddities as sloping piston crowns to suit the angle between the bores and the head. The valves were operated by rockers and, an unusual refinement at this time, the whole mechanism was enclosed in an oil bath. Equally sophisticated, the lubrication of the partitioned engine block separating the rod assembly, clutch and gearbox was via a mechanical pump. The single head for the two cylinders with its sealed casing enclosing the valve gear was fixed in place with eight bolts and was easy to dismantle. Another rarity was the three-speed gearbox with sliding gears, incorporated in the engine block, with the controls passing through the fuel tank and operated by a small crank. The clutch was at the end of the crankshaft, in a casing, and the primary and secondary transmissions were operated by chains in sealed casings.

Two of the most advanced French motorcycles of their time are seen here together in 1992 before a comparative road test: the Louis Clément and my own ABC Gnome & Rhône 400cc flat twin.

On the right side, the throttle; on the left, the front-brake and exhaust-valve lifter levers. The control cables pass through the handlebar tubes.

Two cylinders, but just one cylinder head with a central shaft to drive the OHC and a secondary shaft to drive the ignition magneto.

Jean-Marie Debonneville, the happy owner of the Louis Clément, on his test ride.

A revolutionary, pressed-metal frame

The chassis was every bit as original, with a welded, pressed frame and front suspension as well as a saddle with leaf springs. Just sit back and admire the quality of the sheet-metal work, from the pendular front fork to the rear storage box that also served as a luggage carrier, and not forgetting, of course, the frame itself. Just as modern looking were the interchangeable wheels, made from two aluminium discs with steel rims with quickly detachable spindles and drum brakes, those on the sidecar being coupled to the rear brakes on the bike.

Louis Clément also offered a range of sidecars finished in the same colours as the motorcycle, as well as a sports model, a twin-seater version intended for public-service use, and 'closed-cab' and delivery models. The chassis was made from welded tubes clad in sheet metal enamelled in the same colour as the bike. The braked, aluminium disc wheels were interchangeable with those on the motorcycle. As the instructions pointed out, only one spare wheel was required.

As is so often the case with engineering that is too far ahead of its time, the Louis Clément did not sell well. It cost 3,500 francs on its own or 4,500 francs with a sidecar, compared with a military surplus Harley and sidecar at 3,500 francs.

● ● ● ● Twin-cylinder V-engine at 55°, air cooled – 540cc (62 x 90mm) – Shaft-driven SOHC – Valves and rockers in sealed casing – Automatic lubrication – Magneto ignition – Gearbox in units with three speeds operated by a quadrant on the fuel tank – Foot-operated wet multi-plate clutch on the engine shaft – Kick starting – Primary transmission via a chain and secondary via a chain in a sealed casing with automatic lubrication – Pressed-steel frame – 10-litre fuel tank – Pendular front fork on leaf springs – Drum brakes, rear and sidecar linked – Steel rims and aluminium-disc wheel centres – 26 x 3.00 beaded tyres – 150kg – 75km/h (47mph).

The fuel tank made from two sections joined together encloses the frame. Petrol is on the left and oil on the right, with a plunger pump and a meter to regulate the lubrication drop by drop. The notched lever behind is for changing gear.

The luggage carrier is made from pressed sheet, like the frame, and forms a stowage compartment. The wheels are steel rimmed with aluminium-disc infills. Note the front and rear kickstands and, on the front fork, the very neat tension adjuster for the front brake cable, using a lever attached to an eccentric.

Impressed by the Krieger-Gnädig, famous globe-trotter Robert Sexé bought it after the race from Lövenich, seen here at Mannheim in 1921. This sport version, capable of 100km/h (62mph), is recognisable by its horizontal carburettor.

KRIEGER-GNÄDIG (1921–1926)
The first German motorcycle with shaft transmission

The standard version used by Sexé in 1921 was fitted with an enormous exhaust outlet and a transverse silencer ahead of the engine. The carburettor hung on the end of a curious vertical inlet pipe.

In 1923, BMW introduced a solidly built motorcycle with a flat-twin engine, side valves and shaft transmission that would make its fortune and its reputation. Yet it should not be forgotten that other manufacturers cleared the way for these features, which at the time were much more avant-garde. Such was the case in 1919 with the ABC and its rocker-valve flat twin and the Krieger-Gnädig with its shaft transmission, the first of its type in Germany.

In 1919, at Suhl, in Thuringia, the three Krieger brothers, former military air aces, and the engineer Franz Gnädig, built the first production German motorcycle to offer a shaft transmission, four years before BMW. It was a very modern machine for its time, with an aluminium piston and crankcase, and three-speed gearbox. Using their aviation background, the Krieger brothers also opted for dry-sump lubrication, a most unusual feature on motorcycles at this time. The triangular frame was also ahead of its time, although the same could not be said for the leaf-spring front suspension.

Robert Sexé in 1922 at Neustadt, with the Krieger-Gnädig Sport that he had recently acquired. 'Very heavy (135kg), but very pleasant on a trip', noted Sexé on the back of the photo, 'except when you have to get off and push because of a broken connecting rod!'

Attached to a sidecar around 1924.

Calamity. Not just a broken conrod, but a crash on ice.

A career curtailed

With Germany hit by the crisis in 1922, Krieger-Gnädig joined up with Cito so as to rationalise their respective products. In 1923, Cito was in turn absorbed by the established firm of Allright. An unfortunate combination of circumstances hastened the end of the magnificent KG. Based in Cologne, Allright wanted to concentrate its production in that city, especially as the recent BMW flat twin had made all of its competitors look outdated, despite a half-hearted attempt at modernisation by the engineer Rudi Albert. So the Krieger-Gnädigs disappeared from the Allright catalogue, although production was continued under Paul Henkel's name until 1930.

A change of course

Even before Allright had ceased making the KGs in order to concentrate on bicycles and the supply of parts for other manufacturers (suspension, brakes, etc), the Krieger brothers and Franz Gnädig jumped ship. The brothers reappeared in 1925 with a short-lived Blackburne-engined machine under the Original Krieger brand, while in 1924 Gnädig introduced a new product carrying his name. In 1926, he would join Diamant, which was returning to motorbike production, eventually ending up in the Opel group.

Lövenich, racing driver and agent for Krieger-Gnädig in Mannheim, poses behind the 1921 Cardan Sport 500.

A 1922 Krieger-Gnädig catalogue.

●●●● Single-cylinder, four-stroke, air-cooled engine – 497cc (80 x 99mm) – 10hp at 3,500rpm – Overhead valves, pushrod operated with exposed rockers – Magneto ignition – Manual 3-speed gearbox – Shaft transmission – Triangulated, tubed frame – Front pendular suspension, later parallelogram – Drum brakes – 15-litre fuel tank – 120kg empty weight – 100km/h (62mph).

Another 1922–1923 version, with the two vertical valves readily visible. This time, the exhaust pipe is a rectangular tube.

An advertisement from 1925. The engine now has inclined valves, but the fork hasn't yet been changed.

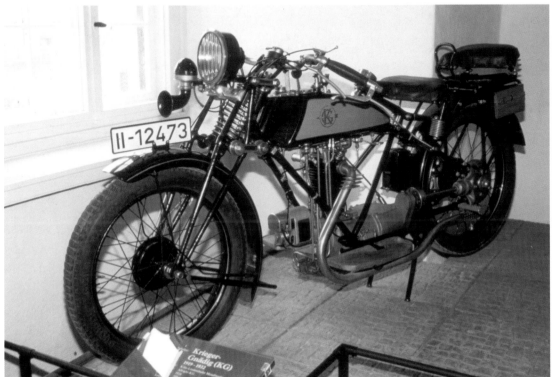

On this final, 1926, version displayed at the Augustusburg Museum in Germany, the front end has swapped its pendular fork bearing on leaf springs for a more-conventional parallelogram girder fork, and the cylinder head, redesigned by the JAP engine company, has inclined valves.

MEGOLA (1921–1925)
Quite a runner

The 1920s were among the craziest years in the history of the motorcycle, with engineers giving free rein to their wildest ideas.

Fritz Cockerell (1889–1965) began his career in aviation, which gave him a penchant for radial engines. His first motorbike, the 1918–1919 Pax, had a three-cylinder version of the type mounted in the rear wheel, but he had a more ambitious idea: a five-cylinder radial in the front wheel! In 1921, he joined up with MEixner and LAndgraf to produce the MeGoLa (a 'G' having mysteriously replaced the initial 'C' of his name), which appears to have been the only front-wheel, rotary, radial-engined motorcycle to have gone into production. (Félix Millet's first five-cylinder wheel of 1889 was mounted on a tricycle, and on the 1895 motorcycle, the same engine was mounted on the rear wheel.)

The advertising claimed: 'The Megola combines the advantages of the car and the motorcycle. It has the power, reliability, convenience and ease of driving of the former, as well as the handling, compactness and low production and running costs of the latter.' Nonetheless, the legendary Megola faced numerous technical problems. Over its short career, from 1922 to 1925, there were five changes of the cylinder type and three of the crankcase, and contrary to the often-quoted production figure of 2,000 models, fewer than 500 were actually turned out, of which around 20 have survived.

The front-mounted five-cylinder radial engine turned in the opposite direction to the wheel and at six times its speed! There was no clutch or gearbox. The crankcase acted as the hub and was driven by the crankshaft via epicyclic gearing. When the engine was running, the only stationary parts were the carburettor on the right and the magneto on the left, which was powered by bevel gearing at the end of the crankshaft.

Thanks to its low centre of gravity, the Megola was stable and very fast, as long as it didn't turn too sharply as the big gyro in the front wheel hardly enhanced the handling! For four years, the five racing versions built accumulated many successes in competitions, even winning the German National Championship in 1924, in which Toni Bauhofer reached 145kph on the Avus circuit in Berlin. His racing Megola, without rear suspension, developed more than 14hp at an engine speed of 4,800rpm (800rpm at the wheel).

The cycle itself consisted of a sheet-steel body, leading-link front suspension and leaf springs, and on the touring version a leaf-spring rear suspension with the seat mounted on the body. It had total loss lubrication with a tank on the left fork and an oil syringe to provide an extra squirt if required.

The Megola is particularly well equipped: petrol gauge, speedometer and ammeter.

A 1923 racing version.

Among its original features were: a main 10- to 12-litre fuel tank in the body, from which fuel could be transferred as needed by a hand pump into a small three-litre tank on the fork; the ability to dismantle the cylinders without removing the spokes and to inflate the special 'open' inner tube without taking the wheel off. The crisis in Germany saw the disappearance of Megola in late 1925, but 10 years later five young German engineers were inspired by this extraordinary machine to create an even crazier one, the Killinger & Freund.

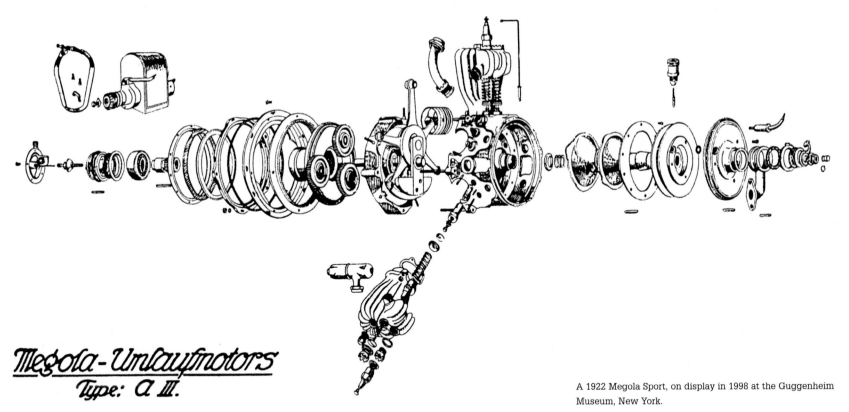

Megola-Umlaufmotors
Type: A III.

A 1922 Megola Sport, on display in 1998 at the Guggenheim Museum, New York.

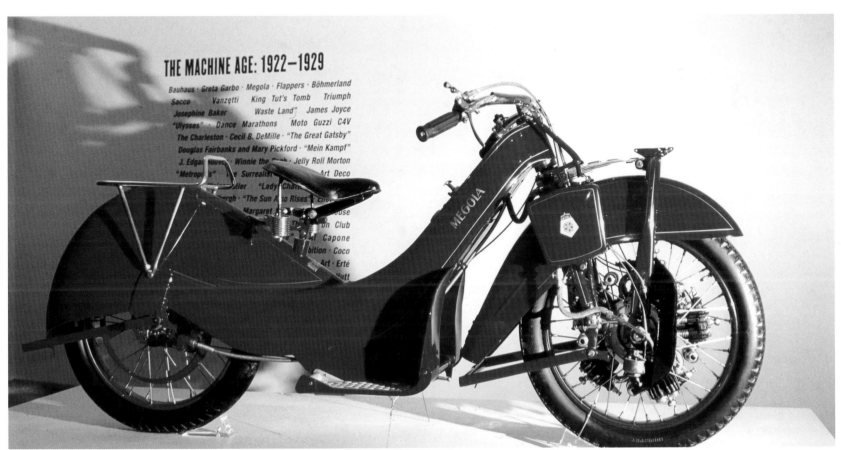

THE MACHINE AGE: 1922–1929

Bauhaus · Greta Garbo · Megola · Flappers · Böhmerland
Sacco   Vanzetti   King Tut's Tomb   Triumph
Josephine Baker   Waste Land"   James Joyce
"Ulysses"   Dance Marathons   Moto Guzzi C4V
The Charleston · Cecil B. DeMille · "The Great Gatsby"
Douglas Fairbanks and Mary Pickford · "Mein Kampf"
J. Edgar   rover · Winnie the   h · Jelly Roll Morton
"Metrop   is"   e Surrealist   Art Deco

The crown wheel of the engine crankcase is driven by an epicyclic gear train and turns in the opposite direction to the crankshaft.

Visible in the centre, the bevel gear on the end of the crankshaft drives the magneto (2:3 ratio).

There are short stub exhaust pipes and the single carburettor is protected by a scoop at hub height, which is extended vertically to form an airbox.

● ● ● ● Rotating, four-stroke, 5-cylinder engine on the front wheel – 640cc (52 x 60mm) – 14hp at 4800rpm (racing) – Side valves – Magneto ignition – Total-loss lubrication – No gearbox or clutch – Driven front wheel – Frame/body in pressed sheet – Leaf-spring suspension, front leading-link, rear swing on leaf springs (touring) – Single drum brake on rear wheel – 110km/h (68mph) (racing version 143kph [89mph]).

Fernand Barbier stands admiringly before his creation, in December 1934.

BARBIER (1934)
A flat-iron dream

I n the France of the 1930s, the papers were full of prototypes and other models teeming with new ideas that had been turned out by small manufacturers in their pursuit of their dream of the ideal motorcycle...

Ungainly and with few aesthetic qualities, the motorcycle produced in 1934 by a certain Mr Barbier, a keen traveller, well illustrates the problems as well as the dreams of motorcyclists of the time: the low-mounted seat allowed the driver to 'pedal' over difficult sections and rest his forearms on his knees (these things had to be considered!) during long journeys. In the absence of any fairings, the low position also afforded protection for the driver, who was well hidden behind his hump-shaped fuel tank. By contrast, the passenger seat was at normal level. You can imagine the bizarre sight – almost worse than on a BMW C1 scooter – presented by the passenger clinging on behind!

A full-sized Meccano model
Barbier made almost everything himself on his strange motorcycle, constructing it around a 500cc Blackburne pushrod engine with internal flywheels, twin-port exhausts and a separate hand-change gearbox.

The front suspension, of a standard girder type, was also, of course, made from flat iron, and the handlebars – no, we're not dreaming! – were fixed under the tripleclamp of the lower fork. Questions might also be asked about the twin exhaust, which was made from straight tubes and spheres. While quite elegant (compared with the rest, at any rate!), the turbulence created in the latter would hardly have favoured gas flow and engine performance.

One dreads to think what it would be like to perch on the high pillion seat – probably terrifying!

Flat strip-metal frame, bolted and riveted; minimal ground clearance, low seat position and tortuous exhaust pipe runs...

The feet are firmly placed, but what about the forearms resting on the knees? Even a quick trip around town would be uncomfortable!

●●●● Blackburne engines

From the late 1920s to the beginning of the 1930s, the British firm Blackburne offered a complete range of four-stroke engines, from 175 to 500cc, that were used by more than 50 manufacturers including, in France, Automoto, Favor, Magnat-Debon, Motobécane, Ravat, Styl'son and Terrot, to name only the best known. In view of the Barbier's supposed weight, it was unlikely to have been the nippiest of the 500s powered by this engine (350cc: bore x stroke 71 x 88mm, 14.7hp at 4,800rpm; 500cc: 81 x 91.8mm, 22hp at 4,800rpm and 28.5hp at 5,800rpm from the racing version). Powerful, reliable and well built, these engines were distinguished by a liveliness that made them formidable engines for hill-climbing races, where they outperformed the JAP engines (also British-made), which were better at climbing at high engine speeds, but not as good at low speeds.

KILLINGER & FREUND (1938)
Modern art

W hile the German Megola from the 1920s with its five cylinders on the front wheel is well enough known, it is unlikely you will have seen the 1938 Killinger & Freund, a remarkable super-Megola.

Until now, historical works have always shown this Killinger & Freund as a drawing, or in small, blurred photographs. *Das Motorrad*, the standard German reference work, contains just a brief note on it from 1938, by Christian Christophe, and while the French national motorcycle weekly, *Moto Revue*, makes mention of it in the same year, the text was actually about the 1922 Megola! It was not until the advent of the internet that Daniel Des Biens, a young Canadian blogger, related the story of how his grandfather had left him some motorbike photos taken in 1945. A few fruitful international exchanges later and there emerged the story of one of the most outrageous prototypes ever built.

In 1935, the young engineer Killinger, along with four other engineers from Munich, joined with the coachbuilder Walter Freund to design the motorcycle of the future, inspired by the famous Megola of 1922, but brought up to date using the latest aerodynamic theory tinged with a more-human aspect!

It took them three years of quite hard work. Like the Megola, the Félix Millet and the Sévitame, this motorcycle was among the select group that the designers had thought out down to the last bolt... and their time was not wasted.

1945 war booty. A bit of a culture shock for a soldier more used to Harleys and Indians. Note the stylish appearance, even down to the details, such as the gear selector pedal. (Daniel Des Biens Archive)

The only Killinger built was appropriated by the Allied forces in 1945, but its memory inspired the sculptor Biebl Wunderlich, who 20 years later created this superb statue that graces Helene Weigel Square in Berlin-Marzahn. (Anne Meuter and Juliette Fayard Photos)

A defiance of convention

Like the Megola that inspired it, which was in production between 1921 and 1925, the Killinger had a radial engine in the front wheel, but on this occasion it was a 600cc, three-cylinder, two-stroke type (presumably borrowed from aeronautical tradition), while the Megola used a five-cylinder, four-stroke engine with side valves. It might, however, be more accurate to describe the Killinger as three-engined rather than three-cylindered, as this remarkable set-up was quite unlike a radial engine. It consisted of three separate crankcases with three crankshafts without flywheels engaging at a tangent with a single flywheel in the central hub casing and incorporating a two-speed, epicyclic gearbox, a clutch, the distributor and the mounting points for the battery-coil ignition... not to mention a drum brake!

The Killinger rescued by the Allied invaders in 1945 was little damaged. The missing front axle cover allows us to see the air intake and the fork mounting, and the other one missing below the tank gives access to the battery and the saddle suspension adjustment. On either side of the front mudguard are the fuel pipe and the gear change cable. (Daniel Des Biens Archive)

Looking superb, just as it appeared to the German readers of *Das Motorrad* in 1938. All it lacks is two little flags on top of the front shock absorbers!

The designers, interviewed in a 1938 issue of *Das Motorrad*, admitted to having even considered including an electric starter, eventually rejecting the idea so as not to put too much weight on the front wheel. Even so, this part of the bike weighed 50kg, although this was not too bad given what was incorporated and it was certainly less than the Megola's five-cylinder wheel, but it was still quite a weight for a front wheel! The three cylinders, in light alloy with iron liners, were fed by a single rotating disc valve and a special carburettor with a needle-less float to avoid its being upset by vibration. The mixture was fed into the three casings, which worked in the standard way.

The cable-operated two-speed gearbox was operated by a foot pedal and used helical gears. The clutch, located between the engine and the gearbox, was of conventional design. As Christian Christophe concluded in *Das Motorrad*: 'This motorcycle has fewer parts than a standard 100cc machine and they are all readily accessible for easy maintenance.'

A remarkable simplicity

Having said all the above, it has to be admitted that, seen from outside, the Killinger's driving wheel appeared remarkably simple. The only mechanical parts, barely visible under the ample fairing, were the cylinder-head fins and the exhaust pipes (three simple cones: the noise must have been phenomenal!) behind the light-alloy wheel spokes. The spokes were so designed that they acted as a sort of cooling fan for the engine.

Unlike the Megola which had to use an open inner tube, the Killinger offered easy replacement thanks to a dismountable rim similar to those used by BMW in long-distance trials and designed by the engineer Josef Stelaer. All that had to be done was to release a safety catch to remove the half rim, followed by the tyre, a Michelin 4.00 x 19in motorcycle special.

Again unlike the Megola, the body, or rather, the frame was not the pressed-steel monocoque that it seemed to be. The designers had indeed intended future models to be made from two half-bodies welded together, but this prototype had a tubed frame clad in steel sheet with a sprung saddle and a streamlined rear mudguard that completely enclosed the wheel. Once you've finished admiring the superb layout of the handlebars, go to the front and try out the suspension provided by a fork that is as curious as it is stylish, with a pressed-sheet support protecting the almost vertical, telescopic, coil-sprung and hydraulically damped legs. The pride of the designers, this arrangement had the advantage of allowing 80mm of suspension without significantly altering the wheelbase.

The sublime aerodynamic bodywork also concealed the rear suspension, which was attached to the base of the frame tube and pivoted on metal/rubber rings. To add to the comfort, there was fully adjustable saddle suspension.

This magnificent piece of sculpture would not have looked out of place in a museum of modern art!

From the 'dove of peace' to the 'final victory'

After lengthy bench testing of the engine, the Killinger, now christened *Friedenstaube* ('dove of peace'), was tried out on the road by its designers, who spent two years working on getting it into production. In 1940, the war put an end to their hopes, while the project, so it is said, had been renamed 'final victory'! The single example that had been built underwent something of an adventure, falling into Allied hands at Suhl in the spring of 1945, where our Canadian friend's grandfather took the photos. Although it doesn't appear on the list of motorcycles seized by the American Army, the Killinger nevertheless was sent to the United States two months before the Red Army took over the Simson factory where it was built. Taken to pieces and stored, it didn't reappear until the 1950s, when it was sold on and preserved in its then condition (without the front and rear wheels) by a collector in Pennsylvania. It is currently undergoing restoration.

The Killinger, here seen mounted on a stand, is on its way to the Salon in late 1938... A pity that the photographer focused on the buildings in the background.

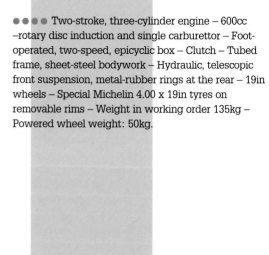

The left side of the front wheel shows how the three crankshafts are positioned at a tangent to the hub, and the way the alloy wheel spokes are arranged to act as ventilators. (Daniel Des Biens Archive)

The right-hand side of the wheel after the detachable rim has been taken off.

The right side of the wheel with the clutch in front of the gearbox and its springs on the outer circumference. Note the use of socket screws to secure the detachable rim and the very short exhaust pipes. (Daniel Des Biens Archive)

●●●● Two-stroke, three-cylinder engine – 600cc –rotary disc induction and single carburettor – Foot-operated, two-speed, epicyclic box – Clutch – Tubed frame, sheet-steel bodywork – Hydraulic, telescopic front suspension, metal-rubber rings at the rear – 19in wheels – Special Michelin 4.00 x 19in tyres on removable rims – Weight in working order 135kg – Powered wheel weight: 50kg.

A fter the war, large-capacity motorcycles were chiefly either German or British. There were one or two French attempts that might have taken up the challenge, of which one of the most remarkable was the Gnome & Rhône/Avions Voisin 500cc Super-Star of 1950.

GNOME & RHÔNE (1950)
Super-Star... for a day!

One can't blame Gnome & Rhône for not having responded to the challenge. Its strange project unveiled at the 1946 Paris Show, the 350 WM with two double pistons, was not followed up. In the meantime, management of the motorcycle division had passed to Avions Voisin, and the engineer in charge of the WM, Igor Troubetzkoy, was surprised to come across the 500 Super-Star at the 1950 Show, having been quite unaware of its existence! The new Avions Voisin brand name borne by Gnome products from September 1949 did not indicate that the brilliant engineer Gabriel Voisin was particularly committed to these motorcycles. It was more prosaically a case of political and financial wheeling and dealing. Nationalised in 1945, Gnome & Rhône became Snecma (*Société National d'Études et de Construction de Moteurs et d'Avions*) and, while its name gave no hint of this, it continued to build motorcycles under the Gnome & Rhône brand name at its Gennevilliers factory. From 1949, production was managed by the Avions Voisin Company, which had recently come under the control of Snecma. The latter, short of cash and having used up all the subsidy granted to it by the state, went back and asked for the same favour, only this time under the name of Avions Voisin.

The new management of the motorcycle department started off with a fresh model, the R4, and two big projects, the Biscooter and the 500 Super-Star, designed, in theory, for the Army.

The first was entirely Gabriel Voisin's baby, while the second was entrusted to Giuseppe Remondini, who was responsible for the Jonghi motorcycle and in particular France's only 125cc machine with overhead cams. Hired by Snecma in September 1948, Remondini stayed with them until 1952. His mission was to create a modern 500cc vertical twin. Although he had originally planned to use gear-driven overhead cams, he adopted pushrod valve gear for the prototypes. Unlike the English twins, traditionally long spoke, the Super-Star used the same 'square' bore and stroke (68 x 68mm) as the pre-war Gnome CV2 and some BMW twins.

In the limelight at the 1950 Paris Salon. As on the Jonghi 250cc two-stroke and 125cc four-stroke SOHC, the fork tubes are just for steering and the shock absorber is in the middle. The forward ends of the two rear shock absorbers can be seen below the engine.

The clutch on the end of the crankshaft on the right, and the magneto on the left, widened the engine considerably. Behind the selector, the small lever operates the gearbox manually.

With very clean lines, the engine block included a four-speed gearbox with the foot-change supplemented by a small manual lever. The one suspect choice, though characteristic of Remondini, was the placing of the clutch at the end of the crankshaft, thus considerably widening the bottom of the engine, a cause of concern during development. The motor-cycle was otherwise superbly equipped: telescopic front suspension with a single central damper between the two fork tubes, Moto Guzzi-style rear suspension with a triangular swingarm and two telescopic struts under the engine block working in tension. Also notable were the interchangeable wheels, their superb alloy hub brakes and the sealed final drive chain casing.

Yet sadly, it was not destined to work out. The civilian population was still pretty hard up in 1950 and the Army, getting cold feet faced with this novelty, ordered 3,000 BMWs, and Gnome & Rhône were not in a financial state to make the necessary investment.

It was a great shame and the magnificent 500 would be the Super-Star of just one Paris Salon, in October 1950. It was planned to produce a 135km/h (84mph) tourer and a 150km/h (93mph) sports version with twin carburettors. In the end, only a few prototypes were built (none of which survive) of a motorcycle that would have been among the most up to date of its time.

Fully and luxuriously equipped: enclosed chain , aluminium plates for the passenger footrests, or a suspended luggage carrier required by the Army and, on the font hub six chain sprocket fixing points to make it interchangeable with the rear wheel.

●●●● Four-stroke, inclined parallel twin – 494cc (68 x 68mm) – crankshaft on four bearings – OHV – One or two carburettors according to the version – Magneto ignition – Four-speed gearbox, a selector on the right and a lever – Primary transmission by helical gears, final drive by enclosed chain – Double-cradle frame – Telescopic front suspension with a central shock absorber, rear swingarm suspension with two spring units under the engine working in tension – 19in interchangeable wheels – Drum hub-brakes with a single cam – 175kg.

The light alloy cylinders and heads are separate castings. This show machine had a single carburettor but a twin-carburettor version gave better performance.

PIETRO VASSENA (1947–1953)
From the bathyscaphe to the two- (or three-) cylinder Rumi

It was by no means a coincidence. Rumi, a manufacturer that had always specialised in castings for the shipbuilding industry and whose trademark was a ship's anchor, owed the idea of its famous little two-cylinder machine to the well-known Italian designer of the bathyscaphe, Pietro Vassena.

Pietro Vassena, in his work overalls, oversees the preparation of his famous C3 bathyscaphe of 1947–1948. (Angelo Vassena Archive)

It might as well be said straight away that in the hall of fame of off-the-wall engineers — and by this I mean true geniuses — those who have come up with the most unlikely inventions and sometimes revolutionised the world with things that no-one else would even have dared think about, Pietro Vassena has pride of place, along with people like Granville Bradshaw, Marcel Violet and Lino Tonti, to mention just a few from long list of motorcycle innovators alone. Born in 1897, Vassena served in the First World War as a motorcycle courier and it is without any doubt this experience that inspired him in 1923 to design an engine that could be fitted to a bicycle, followed by proper 100cc and 125cc motorcycles for the Faini brand and available in touring, sport and ladies' or priests' versions. This initial project made use of one of Vassena's principal ideas, with a horizontal-cylindered, two-stroke engine. (From a marketing point of view, what an excellent idea to turn out from Lecco, only a few kilometres from the Moto Guzzi factory, a lightweight motorcycle with a similar appearance to the already very well-known horizontal-cylindered Guzzi 500.)

Also in 1923, Pietro Vassena founded the enterprise that would be his principal source of income: the design and construction of outboard engines for boats. In November 1925, under his own brand name, he introduced a 125cc motorcycle very like the one designed for Faini, with a magneto now built into the crankcase. Bore and stroke were identical at 53 x 56mm, and the separate gearbox soon gave way to a combined engine-block/two-speed gearbox. In 1928, the Vassena finished fourth on the Lario race circuit behind the GDs and MMs, the big names in their category. The Vassena, though enlarged to 175cc, was little heard of after this and disappeared from the scene for good in 1930, as its creator turned to the joys of submarines.

The 1953 Carniti Automotoscooter. Almost conventional-looking from this angle. (Vittorio Tessera Archive)

An amazing transmission with two telescopic drive shafts ending in conical friction rollers! The drive ratio is changed by moving the lever, causing the roller supports to slide from the periphery towards the centre of the disc wheel. Another lever works the clutch by causing the rollers to pivot. In the black and white photo, you can see that there is only one carburettor for the three cylinders. (Giorgio Sarti; Vittorio Tessera Archive)

The first three-speed Rumi seen at the 1950 Milan Show.

The inventor of the Rumi

Vassena returned to motorcycles indirectly in 1949. Having made a small two-stroke vertical twin engine in 1946 for the Volpe baby car – which in the event was never produced by the manufacturers – he signed an agreement with his friend Donnino Rumi, who owned a foundry at Bergamo, to design a lightweight motorcycle. The first prototype was based on the vertical twin for the baby car and installed on an Amisa motorcycle frame. The engine was then completely redesigned, retaining just its internal dimensions and its deflector pistons inherited from Vassena's outboard engines. The cylinders were now horizontal with rotary induction through the drive shaft. Officially branded Rumi, the engine was shown for the first time at the 1949 Milan Show, still with a borrowed cycle frame.

It then went into production, losing on the way its rotary feed in favour of a standard feed with a third port. Its designer, disinclined in principle to work with the production engineers, broke off his collaboration with Rumi.

Vassena next approached the Carniti Company at Oggiono, granting them production of his outboard engines, which were distributed under the Elios brand. It was while in the Carniti fold that he made a return to motorcycles in 1953.

The 1953 Carniti Automotoscooter: three cylinders, two driveshafts and more

Was it while suffering from the staggers that Pietro Vassena designed his Automotoscooter, displayed at the 1953 Milan Show? It was a machine quite unlike any other, both in its appearance and engineering.

For the engine, Vassena took his inspiration from that designed three years earlier for the Rumi, adding a cylinder and thus creating a three-in-line two-stroke engine, then considered unorthodox. With the bore and stroke remaining the same as on the Rumi, 42 x 45mm, a very compact 187cc unit resulted, with a power output, not unreasonable for the time, of 12hp. You can imagine the noise it must have made. It was not so much in the engine but in the transmission where the Carniti Tre's greatest originality lay. Convinced that a scooter had to be automatic, Vassena had perfected the idea of the variable friction drive used on the Ner-a-Car (United States 1921) and the Mondiale (Belgium 1923): thus was born the Variomatic, inventing both the name and the system. Bevel gears at the rear of the engine transmitted the power to not just one, but two shafts, on each side of the rear disc wheel. Each shaft ended in a conical rubber roller. Wedged between the two rollers, the wheel was friction driven and the length of the telescopic shafts could be adjusted by a handle facing the driver, thereby changing the transmission ratios. Here, you had to take care, because there was also another long handle on the other side of the central tunnel, between the driver's legs, that automatically lowered the central kickstand whose arms were fitted with small wheels to make manoeuvring the bike easier.

Three cylinders, twin-shaft transmission, Variomatic... what else could one ask for? Well, an appearance as bewitching as it was original with a revolutionary footrest arrangement at the front from the great car coachwork designer Ghia, as seen a couple of years earlier on the Ducati Cruiser.

The outstandingly stylish bodywork was designed by Ghia, and the shape of the rear end has similarities to the Ducati Cruiser, from the same stable. (Giorgio Sarti)

With the rear side panel raised, you can see the wonderful complexity of the three-cylinder Automotoscooter. The entire engine/transmission unit is suspended, on two springs, with friction dampers at the rear. Behind the cylinders, you can see the manual starter handle. (Giorgio Sarti; Vittorio Tessera Archive)

The petrol tank rises between two levers, one to lower the centrally placed kickstand (with its small wheels!) and the other to change gear. (Giorgio Sarti)

Carniti 150 Flat twin 1953

Starting with no preconceived ideas, Pietro Vassena worked in concert with Carniti on his three-cylinder two-stroke, his four-stroke single and an amazing 150cc, two-stroke flat twin of which just a few examples were built. The first version was the most conventional. The small IFA-style flat twin, fed by two carburettors and fitted with shaft transmission was mounted in a double cradle tube frame that ran in front of the cylinders. The typically Italian rear swing suspension worked from a pair of springs concealed in the two tubes below the engine.

Probably too conventional, the little 150cc was totally transformed for the second version, which was named 'Faro Girevole' after the moving headlight. The fuel tank was extended forwards enclosing the fork, with the front part holding the curved headlight lens, inside which the headlight itself turned. The engine was completely revised with smoother-shaped crankcases, which likewise were extended forwards where the kick-start was located, which was operated by pushing downwards. The inlet manifold fitted into the crankcase and there was now just a single carb facing the underside of the fuel tank. Also new was the straight-tube double-cradle frame, which now passed above the cylinders with, at the rear, a very neat double loop in the tubes. While of magnificent appearance, it was unfortunately condemned in advance thanks to its high cost relative to the feeble 8hp of the engine.

Like the Automotoscooter, the Carniti flat twin displayed the feathered cap of the Italian Army corps in which Vassena served. (Vittorio Tessera Archive)

Carniti 175 four-stroke scooter 1954

It is odd that while Pietro Vassena's most fanciful motorcycle inventions conquered the Salons and the press, the most realistic project that he created for Carniti, in the mid-1950s, remained a secret and, unless I am much mistaken, never received credit in the media. The other side of the coin is that we know little more about it than what can be seen in photos. The compact rear end incorporated a fine vertical, single-cylinder, four-stroke of 175cc with overhead valves and forced-air cooling under an attractive cast-aluminium casing. The chief novelty was the electric starter, powered by two large batteries on the left side. Gear change was via a foot pedal on the right-hand side, while the brake was operated by another foot pedal at the front on the left. The bodywork, also by Ghia, bore Vassena's signature mark, the *Bersagliera*, a feathered hat as worn by the Army unit in which the engineer had served.

The first version of the Carniti 150 flat twin is conventional having a double cradle below the engine. The front of the engine had a hand starter like that on the three-cylinder version. (Vittorio Tessera Archive)

Undeniable style, but hardly conventional.
(Giorgio Sarti)

It was all change on the second development in 1953. The engine had a kick-start and the upper frame tubes went in a straight line from the steering head to the pivot point of the rear suspension's swingarm. (Giorgio Sarti)

As simple as it is elegant: an engine-transmission swing arm with two shock absorbers in the horizontal tubes below. (Giorgio Sarti)

The Final Vassenas

Vassena didn't send Carniti to the wall, but did show himself to be rather more reasonable and practical with his next client, a group of entrepreneurs from Lecco called Industria Motori Ossana who had decided to invest in motorised two-wheelers, which were much in demand at the time. Pietro Vassena produced a superb 175 for them in 1954, featuring a suspended engine block with aluminium single arm and integrated shaft drive pivoting under a no less superb cast-aluminium frame. In recognition of the expedition led by the Italian climbers Lacedelli and Compagnoni who, on 31 July 1954, became the first to reach the summit of the 8,611m K2 on the Chinese–Pakistan border, the motorcycle was christened K2. However, this final project was also destined to get no further than the prototype stage.

150cc for a two-stroke flat twin of 8hp... The engine was superb, but the project was not financially viable.
(Giorgio Sarti)

Called 'Faro girevole' the headlamp swivelled wth the steering inside a forward extension of the fuel tank.
(Giorgio Sarti)

Classic, if you don't look too closely; the 1954 175 K2 showed wonderfully simple lines. (Giorgio Sarti)

Admire the engine's clean lines and the care taken over details. (Giorgio Sarti)

The whole of the rear part of the 175 K2 was made from aluminium cast in sand moulds. As with the Carniti 150 flat twin, the entire power unit was a pivoting swingarm, but the transmission shaft is now enclosed in a single arm. (Giorgio Sarti)

●●●● The journey of a productive, eclectic genius

1923	Customisable bicycle engines, Faini 125cc and two- or three-cylinder outboard engines.
1925	125 motorbike under the Vassena brand.
1932	Invented 'water skis'.
1934	Autogas gas producer and various petrol-substitute systems.
1938	First underwater experiments.
1942	Built the Delfino torpedo, confiscated by the US Navy in 1944.
1943	C3 bathyscaphe project.
1946	Helios 33cc, 1hp outboard motor.
1948	First C3 tests and record 412m dive in Lake Como.
1953	Three motorcycle projects for Carniti.
1954	New propeller design for the Riva boats; improvements to the Beretta 9mm pistol; gun-barrel lubrication system; injection system for making terracotta pots and vases.
1955	New design for a bicycle gear change; transparent, Plexiglas clock.
1956	Coupling system for two bikes; single-electrode spark plug (patent sold to MV Agusta); anti-hail rocket with a range of 300km (causing a diplomatic incident with Switzerland).
1958	Fiat 500 engine converted into an outboard motor, with alloy propeller mounting; constructed the Grillo, half-autogyro, half-car, with a 240hp engine.
1960	Design for the Minibike produced by Go-Kart.
1967	Pietro Vassena passes away at Lecco.

A very rare meeting of the family of Pietro Vassena models, all preserved by his son, the power boat racing legend Angelo Vassena. From left to right: the Automotoscooter, 'Faro girevole' 150 flat twin and the K2 175 of 1953. (Giorgio Sarti)

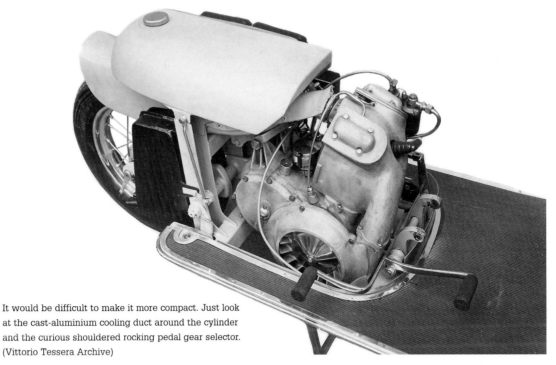

It would be difficult to make it more compact. Just look at the cast-aluminium cooling duct around the cylinder and the curious shouldered rocking pedal gear selector. (Vittorio Tessera Archive)

Of classic appearance seen from the front, the Carniti scooter is dated only by its spoked wheels. However, it does have flashing indicators, a rarity on European two-wheelers at the time. (Vittorio Tessera Archive)

The rear body lifted from the front, giving quick access to the engine. (Vittorio Tessera Archive)

Two big six-volt batteries and a proper electric starter. (Vittorio Tessera Archive)

As with most current scooters, the IMN makes use of an engine/swingarm unit. The pivot point is just behind the cylinders. (François Kiéné Collection)

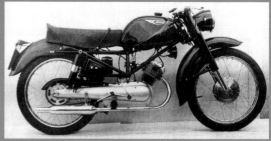

The IMN Baio 100 uses the same cycle part as its big twin-cylinder brother.

IMN ROCKET 200 (1956)
A famous father

Transmission was via a shaft with a tiny casing for the bevel gears. No universal joint was needed as the transmission formed a solid unit with the engine. (François Kiéné Collection)

Who could resist such engineering? Technology to drool over, Italian to die for – and unique. Even more prestigious was the origin of this beautiful newcomer. The IMN Rocket was designed by none other than Carlo Giannini, one of the greatest engineers in the history of Italian motorcycling, who could justly be considered the inventor of the modern racing motorcycle.

The story starts in 1923. The two young students, Remor and Giannini, had just gained their engineering degrees from the University of Rome and managed to persuade Giovanni Bonmartini to give financial backing to their somewhat preposterous idea to build a transverse-engined, four-cylinder motorcycle. Thus in 1926 was born the GRB (Gianni, Remor, Bonmartini), a revolutionary racing bike with four transverse in-line cylinders, a 500cc engine with shaft-driven single OHC (followed by twin OHC in 1929) and chain-driven final transmission. It was built by Opra in 1927 and clocked at 170kph at 7,200rpm.

The Rondine as founder of present-day racing

In 1934, Giannini, who had been promoted to technical director of the Compania Nazionale Aeronautica (CNA) in Rome, decided to revisit the idea of a four-cylinder racing bike. It would be christened 'Rondine' after a tiny monoplane built by CNA in 1922 with an ABC 400cc engine and piloted by the famous Donati. (It's a small world!) Designed by Giannini and Remor, the CNA Rondine, introduced in 1935, was a 500cc bike with four inclined cylinders, liquid cooling, DOHC and supercharged induction, with a pressed-steel perimeter frame. It won its first victory at the 1935 Tripoli Grand Prix. In streamlined form, it took the first outright Italian speed record at 244km/h (152mph).

Its career under the CNA banner went no further, with the company being bought by Caproni who showed no interest in the project. In the spirit of keeping things within the aviation industry and after a brilliant demonstration at Montlhéry, the four-cylinder Rondine was offered to Gnome & Rhône, who turned it down, then to Moto Guzzi and Norton. The project finally ended up at Gilera, with the success that we all know. Completely revised with the assistance of Gilera's celebrated engineer-driver and sporting director, Piero Taruffi, and provided with the latest type of perimeter tubular frame and swing rear suspension, the Rondine Gilera created the archetype for the modern racing bike, a sort of Yamaha M1 of its day, which in its streamlined form would reach 274km/h (170mph)!

From Moto Guzzi to MV Agusta

Giannini then went briefly to Moto Guzzi for just long enough to produce the Tarf with Piero Taruffi, an innovative record-breaking four-wheeler comprising two fuselages. For a complete change, Giannini next designed the four-cylinder, in-line Guzzi 500 of 1952, another fine original with gear-driven OHC, indirect mechanical injection, shaft transmission and Ducati-style trellis tubular frame. It produced a claimed 54hp at 9,000rpm and a top speed of 230kph, but its short career was distinguished by just a single win, in the 1953 German Grand Prix with an average speed of 176km/h (109mph), and in 1955 it gave way to the Guzzi 500 V8. Fickle, Giannini moved on to MV Agusta where, in the same year, he designed a 300cc, two-cylinder machine with twin DOHC, which remained in prototype form, but gave rise to a fabulous trellis-framed racing 350 in 1957.

Going home

Perhaps Giannini, now aged 63, was feeling homesick for his native Rome. He returned south and joined Industria Meccanica Napoletana (IMN), a small Neapolitan company, which at that time was the only one of the 157 Italian manufacturers that was based south of Rome and with a very limited production between 1950 and 1958. It began in 1950 with the Mosquito-engined 38cc Paperino, followed in 1953 by the Baio with its 100cc four-stroke engine and pressed-steel frame. Giannini capped all this with the 100cc, single-cylinder Baio and the 200cc flat twin Rocket displayed at the 1956 Milan Show. The two machines were very similar, sharing the same trellis tubular upper frame from which the engine-swingarm unit was suspended. It's true that the IMN Rocket flat twin was not turned out in any numbers, but this stylish 200cc (52 x 46.5mm) with rocker valves and four-speed gearbox put out 11hp at 6,000rpm, weighed 120kg and could reach 120km/h (75mph).

Only a handful of IMN Rocket flat twins were built and this is the sole remaining example. (François Kiéné Collection)

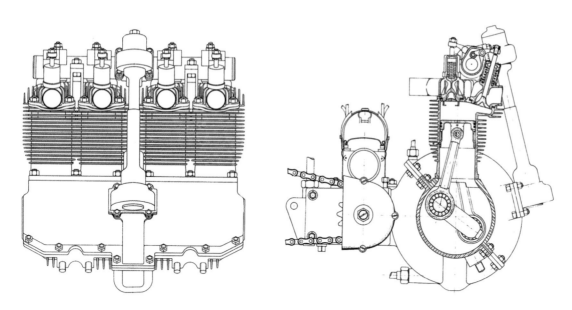

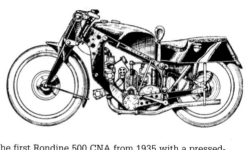

The first Rondine 500 CNA from 1935 with a pressed-metal frame.

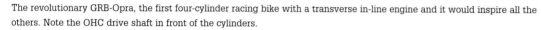

The revolutionary GRB-Opra, the first four-cylinder racing bike with a transverse in-line engine and it would inspire all the others. Note the OHC drive shaft in front of the cylinders.

More than 80 years later, the Gilera Rondine's engine remains the archetype of all modern in-line four-cylinder engines.

The fabulous Gilera Rondine 500, four-cylinder, with DOHC and liquid cooling, in its 1939 version with a supercharger and tubular frame. With streamlined fairings it could exceed 270km/h (168mph).

In 1952, relying on no preconceived ideas, Giannini, the father of the first transverse, four-cylinder, in-line engined racing bike, designed this revolutionary in-line four-cylinder machine for Moto Guzzi. In-line with the frame, its engine featured fuel injection.

The 1957 MV Agusta 350 designed by Giannini during his brief sojourn at the Gallarate factory.

JAPANESE CLONES

Rikuo (1937-1960): Harley's natural child from Japan

The huge 1939 Rikuo 1200cc with a driven-wheel sidecar attached: 500kg, 2.76m long, 1.67m wide and 1.08m high! (Costantino Frontalini, Sidecar Museum, Cingoli)

The Rikuo 1200 from the rear with its shaft transmission and universal-jointed shaft leading to the sidecar's wheel. This was one of the earliest driven-wheel sidecars. (Costantino Frontalini, Sidecar Museum Cingoli)

In its early days, Japanese production was mainly inspired by German or British bikes. Yet the ultimate dream of Japanese motorcyclists originated in the United States, with its Harley-Davidsons, despite their astronomical price and their size, which was suited neither to the jungle of local roads nor to the stature of the inhabitants. In 1923, the American Alfred Rich Child, who had been appointed as the authorised Harley representative for Japan, China, Manchuria and Korea, set up the first Harley-Davidson agency in Japan. These prestigious machines were soon to be found equipping police forces, the Army and even the Imperial Guard.

Harley made in Japan

Unfortunately for Harley, after the 1929 crash, the US market was at rock bottom and sales were collapsing in Japan as well, where prices were reaching unattainable heights: 1,890 yen for a 1,200cc when the average worker earned 90 yen a month! The Milwaukee plant, which was working at just 10% of its potential output with fewer than 4,000 machines made in 1932, was persuaded by Child to grant production licences for the only time in its history in an attempt to bring down production costs.

The Rikuo Airstone Company ('Rikuo' means 'king of the road' in Japanese), a subsidiary of the Sankyo Seiyako Corporation, was established in late 1932 in the suburbs of Tokyo. The first 750 was built there in 1934 and when

War in China, 1936: the Chinese roads were even rougher than those in Japan and both Rikuo and Kurogane were quick to modify their 750 and 1,200cc bikes with raised engines in 1937, later adding a disengageable, driven-wheel sidecar. (Costantino Frontalini Archive)

A return to civilian life for a 1953 1,200cc Rikuo.

machine tools were brought in from the United States, Rikuo turned out the first 1,200cc entirely made in Japan, in 1935.

The happy relationship lasted just a brief moment. Rikuo was nationalised that very same year and things went irretrievably sour in 1937 when Harley refused Child permission to build the new OHV 'knucklehead' 750. Japan was militarising and put a stop on all licence payments and forcibly sent Child back to the US without any compensation paid to Harley-Davidson. Ford, Chrysler and GM were to suffer the same fate between then and 1939.

Rikuo: bikes, sidecars and torpedoes

Despite this, Rikuo continued to produce 1200s for the Japanese Army that were virtually identical to the Harleys. In 1936, they even modified the original model by producing a 1,200cc with a raised engine and, a year later, a sidecar version with a (disengageable) driven wheel that would be used in the war against China. Similar models were built, also with driven-wheel sidecars, by Kurogane and Aikoku, both part of the JAC group.

After delivering close to 18,000 machines since the start of hostilities with China, Rikuo responded to military requirements by abandoning motorcycle production in 1942 to concentrate on making torpedoes.

The company returned to motorcycles after the war with

a 750 in 1947, followed by a 1,200cc with side valves in 1950. In 1953, the range was complemented by a single-cylinder OHV 350 with shaft drive evidently inspired by BMW, which was replaced in 1958 by a 250cc version. At this time, Rikuo was producing about 2,000 motorcycles a year and with the largest engine capacity of any in Japan.

In 1960, Rikuo finally set about modernising its old side-valve, V-twin with the OHV 750 RX shown here. Unfortunately, it didn't get beyond the prototype stage. Japan, which had set out to conquer the US reopened its doors to genuine Harley-Davidsons and Rikuo closed its doors for good in 1962.

A 1958 750 Rikuo on show at the 1973 Tokyo Show.

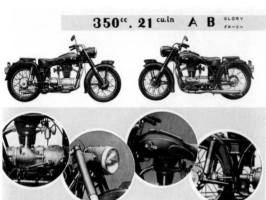

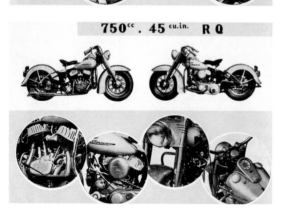

This rare and sumptuous 1960 prototype RX 750 was to be the last Rikuo. Japan, aiming to eventually conquer the US market, opened its doors to the real Harleys. (Asama Memorial Cottage)

1954 Rikuo catalogue.

● ● ● ● Four-stroke, twin-cylinder V-engine at 45° – 747cc (70 x 97mm) – OHV – Cast iron cylinders, aluminium heads – Dry sump – Foot operated four-speed box – Fully enclosed drive chain – Single downtube cradle frame – Telescopic front suspension and swingarm at the rear – 5.00 x 16in tyres – Single-cam drum brakes – 1,500mm wheelbase – 230kg.

Japan took Germany as its model in the motorcycle field, as well as in many others, and BMWs were much emulated there during the 1950s. Some were slavish copies, like the 1956 BIMs (even the name was an admission and they even reproduced the emblem on the fuel tank). The DSKs were also copies (but they did have the maker's blessing); the Tsubasas and the final Rikuo 250s were also very much inspired by BMW, but were rather more than mere copies; finally, between 1964 and 1968, there was the Lilac R92 500, a sad swansong for one of the most outstanding Japanese brands.

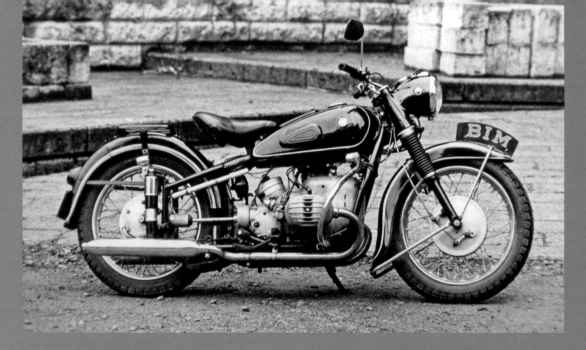

Playing spot the difference between this 1957 BIM 500 and the 1954 BMW R51/3 would be a waste of time! You'd think that BMW had sold its patterns to Japan when it brought out its redesigned R50/2 range with Earles fork in 1955.

The 1955 DSK type A25 was a perfect clone of the R25. Note, however, that it is fitted with flashers, an accessory that very early became obligatory in Japan. (Asama Memorial Cottage)

Ersatz BMWs [1953-1968]

The Daito Seiko Company (DSK) is a special case, as the Tokyo firm, which held sway from 1954 to 1959, had obtained a licence from BMW to build replicas as long as they did not export them to South Asia and, especially, Europe. The DSK A25, like the A50 a copy of the R51/3, was in all points identical to the BMWs of the time. Even the blue, white and black logo was an unmistakeable reminder of the Munich firm. In passing, it is worth recording that DSK had considerable racing success before its factory was destroyed by fire in 1959.

The official models

The oddest thing is that the DSKs were not the only BMW copies in Japan. In the latter half of the 1950s, BIM also turned out identical models and they, too, bore a similar logo to the Munich company's design, yet it is not known whether there was any official agreement between the two companies.

The others

Other makes, such as Rikuo, Tsubasa and later Lilac with its final model, used mechanical parts very much influenced by BMW, yet without being outright copies and at least their appearance was fundamentally different.

Rikuo was less of an imitator than it might appear and after burning its bridges with Harley-Davidson, whose models it had been building under licence, it attempted to relaunch itself in 1953 with a 350. They were not content to take their inspiration directly from the BMW 250s, and the 350s were quite different, both in their general appearance and their 76 x 76mm engine. It was produced up until 1958 and the 1955 version pictured here weighed 170kg, had an output of 16hp and a speed of 100km/h (62mph). Tsubasa (a subsidiary of Daihatsu, which is still in business) arrived later on the scene, in 1959, with the GC 250, which would turn out to be its last model. The internal mechanics appear to be very similar to those of the R25, including the dimensions, but the cycle part and the trim are entirely original.

A bad end

This overview of the Japanese BMW copies ends with Lilac and its R92 produced between 1964 and 1968 and sold in the United States under the name of Marusho, with even an electric-starter version, known as the Magnum Electra. A pale copy of the BMW, it was such a shame that the maker should finish in this way. Lilac had been one of the most inventive and original manufacturers in Japan with its single-cylinder, shaft-transmission 90–250ccs and a whole series of superb two-cylinder transverse V shaft-drive models. It was only with this final model that the manufacturer, financially on its knees, gave up on its usual, original productions in an attempt to retrieve the situation with an ersatz BMW.

At the head of the row, the 1956 DSK A50, a perfect and legal copy of the BMW R51/3. Everything was made in Japan and branded DSK, like the drums brake. (Asagiri Museum, Mount Fuji)

The 1957 BIM catalogue merely confirms that it was a complete copy; the only difference being the Japanese carburettors and the direction indicators.

The final DSK catalogue before the factory went up in flames in 1959. The type AB 250, introduced in Japan in 1958, came from Germany as the BMW R26.

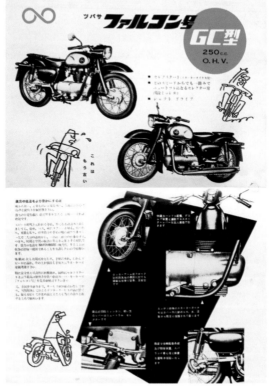

BMW technology, but there was also true originality in this 1959 Tsubasa GC 250. (Asagiri Museum, Mount Fuji)

On this 1964 R92 only the fuel tank remains of the Lilac's original features. It was sold principally in the United States under the Marusho brand. (Asagiri Museum, Mount Fuji)

DU JAPON...
les Sensationnelles
500 LILAC

R 92 A KICK-STARTER : PRIX
R 92 A DEMARREUR ELECTRIQUE : PRIX

IMPORTATEUR : Société Nouvelle LADEVEZE et Cᵉ
6, rue de Marlioze - 95 - Argenteuil

The special talent of the Japanese has often consisted in taking inspiration from an original and making an even better copy. This is the case with the Rikuo 350 AB Glory from 1955 to 1956, which was more up to date than its German inspiration.

Two Lilac R92s were imported into France by Ladeveze in December 1967, but the manufacturer's bankruptcy that same month put an end to further hopes of selling it.

Virtually ready for production that would never happen. This is the competition, a prototype Kawasaki 500cc with single OHC and two valves, being shown off by the test staff in the yard at the factory in 1973.

YAMAHA XT 500 PROTOTYPE (1973)

The XT, predecessor of the XT 500

On display at the 1975 Paris Show, and marketed from February 1976, the Yamaha XT 500 was to change the course of motorcycle history. The revolution had been brewing for more than two years at Yamaha, Kawasaki and doubtless, Honda. The difficulties of developing such an engine and the enormous financial risk involved in such a new concept discouraged some of the early attempts. Only Yamaha persevered, with the success that we all know.

Thank you America and your anti-pollution laws! Since the beginning of the 1970s, the idea had been around of four-stroke engines for trail and enduro bikes. Honda, the big specialist in valve engines, set the ball rolling in 1972 with its fine 250 XL. It was the first large-production four-stroke trail bike. Kawasaki, keen to replace its two-stroke, 350 Big Horn that was very popular in the US, would develop a prototype four-stroke 450cc and then a 500cc in 1973, but abandoned the project after concern about vibration generated by the big single. It would be 1983 before the KL 500 appeared. Always on the lookout for new trends and under pressure, like other manufacturers, from its American partners, Yamaha charged one of its engineers, Oshiro-san, with developing a big four-stroke off-road bike. Although the only likely market was the desert racing then in vogue in the US, right from the start the team had in mind a trail version and perhaps even a road bike. The gestation of the XT and SR was under way and it would be long and hard.

The engineers' nightmare in their own words

This is the picture painted by Shiro Nakamura, entrusted with the engine development on the XT 500 and whose first motorcycle project this was: 'The piston was too heavy. We had piston seizure which caused damage and countless problems. The least one could say was that we seriously lacked experience with four-strokes. The cylinder broke even in the middle, so we added bracing pillars from the head down to the crankcase. To save weight and make use of technology with which we were already familiar, instead of using a one-piece crankshaft or automobile-type assembled connecting rods, we used a built-up crankshaft, which was more compact and cheaper to produce, and a roller big-end bearing, which required only low-pressure lubrication. Even so, the development took much longer than anticipated. The XT, which should have been on sale in 1975, didn't arrive in the showrooms until 1976.' According to Shunji Tanaka, who had left Yamaha's car department (he'd worked on the Toyota 2000 GT and the competition-version engine of the Toyota 7) in order to bring his experience of four-stroke engines to the motorcycle, 'The biggest problem was the damaging effect of vibration, particularly in the crankshaft bearings. However, we never tried a counter-balanced shaft

system. Our other main preoccupation was difficulty in starting and the problem of kick back. One of our directors actually got quite a nasty sprain while kick-starting a pre-production model and it was as a consequence of this incident that we equipped the XT 500's cylinder head with a small inspection window at the SOHC end, which made it possible to move the piston so as to avoid the kick on compression. Later, we perfected the system by adopting an automatic decompressor.' It is said that the test people recorded a lot of crashes and over-revving during the development of the XT and TT, as in the absence of any other means of comparison, they ran alongside BSA Victor big singles with a right-sided foot gear change and the XT with the gear change pedal on the left side!

A surprising success in Europe

The TT and XT, restyled by Leopold Tartarini, were finally rolled out in late 1975 and met with great success in the United States, but those responsible for the European market, T. Tamada, technical director of Yamaha Europe, and Rodney Gould, representing Product Planning, could

see no future for the project in their area. 'We'll not sell more than a few dozen,' was Rodney Gould's opinion. The famous road racer was not entirely wrong, but he was speaking only on behalf of Great Britain, which was long to cold-shoulder this model in the belief that it represented an undesirable return to the numerous vicissitudes of its own thumpers of the past. In the Latin countries and even in Germany, the reception was quite different. Furthermore, the big single-cylinder bike created quite an aura for itself, even with its faults. In France, the XT became something of a phenomenon, with 980 sold in 1976, 1,593 in 1977, 3,982 in 1980 (its best year) and 17,840 in total from 1976 to 1989. The XT did even better in Germany with 24,750 sold between 1977 and 1990, although here it was soon eclipsed by the SR 500, which sold 37,330 between 1978 and 1993. The English, put off by their experience of their own single-cylinder motorbikes were in no mood to try again and bought only 3,109 XTs between 1976 and 1988. Over its 13-year career from 1976 to 1989, 62,600 XT 500s were sold in Europe (out of a total of 196,000 big, four-stroke, single-cylinder Yamaha models).

The first prototype versions of the XT 500 had chain-driven twin overhead camshafts, an oil-cooled cylinder head and a one-piece crankshaft, although a built-up type was later adopted, along with a single OHC.

To increase the stiffness of the upper part of the engine, bracing pillars joined the cylinder head to the engine casing. Note the size of the front brake!

NOVEL
CONCEPTS

BÖHMERLAND

LIEBISCH MOTOR

The 1937 three-seater prototype 600cc Böhmerland for the
Czech Army. (Drawing by Yves Campion)

WOODEN MOTORCYCLES (1895-2010)
The Pinocchio

I t's not just in toys and on roundabouts that we find wooden motorcycles. Indeed, it might even be said that the majority of motorcycles built have been wooden ones that then came to life, just like Pinocchio, the puppet in Carlo Collodi's tale.

According to legend, the first wooden motorcycle was made in Germany in 1885 by Gottlieb Daimler. It was not in fact *the* first motorbike, but the first prototype of a wooden frame with two large wheels and a pair of stabiliser wheels, created for the sole object of testing the fabulous new four-stroke engine invented in 1864 by Beau de Rochas. The first true motorcycle designed as such, then built and tested in Paris between 1864 and 1871 was the steam-powered Michaux-Perreaux whose wheel rims were the only wooden part.

Ash Deltabox Frame

By sheer chance, it was in Germany that the only three other working wooden motorcycles that are known about were built. The first, in 1923, was a Bekamo (soon replaced by a version with a steel frame), followed in the same year by the MFB, made in Hamburg and shown at the Leipzig Fair.

The arguments put forward by the engineer Hugo Ruppe were highly technical: the material chosen, ash, already had a sound reputation in marine construction as well as in aviation for its strength and its ability to absorb vibration and it had been used in these two fields for key structures. The MFB's design was particularly stylish with nickel-steel straps riveted and bolted to the ash frame pieces, which linked each end of the frame and the fork. Sadly, the MFB was just a flash in the pan, having disappeared by 1924. No example of this first generation seems to have survived.

However, it reappeared that same year under the banner of a furniture maker named Hoco from Minden, in Westphalia, without anyone knowing what links they had with MFB. Several engine options were offered, in two- and four-stroke versions, up to 250cc. A fuel tank and a toolbox were set between the frame pieces and metal plates protected the driver's legs from oil splashes and channelled cooling air. Hoco survived until 1928 before going under in the German financial crisis.

The 1885 Daimler. The first prototype of a wooden-framed motorbike, it managed to travel 3km in 1886.

Alex Kow, celebrated for his designs for Panhard, Hotchkiss, Bugatti and various Delahayes, also had a go at the scooter with Monet-Goyon's Starlett and then the Dolina in 1957. Seen here is the wooden mock-up of an improved Dolina that was never produced.

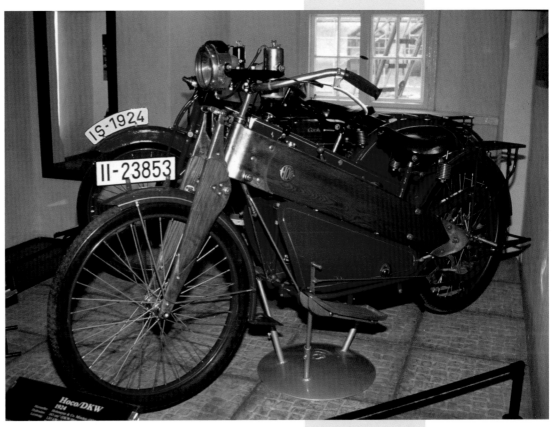

What could be more logical than a furniture maker building a motorbike out of wood? This is the 1924 Hoco. (Augustusburg Museum; Didier Ganneau)

A mock-up of the FZ 750cc five-valve engine made by the Yamaha factory in 1984.

They all start out in wood

These early examples apart, practically all motorbikes see their origin in some sort of wooden form: not only casting moulds, but also complete bodywork formers used to shape the panelling. Computer-assisted design has quietly taken over and models made from expanded polystyrene or resin, shaped by robots guided by the designer's drawing now usually replace the hand-made wooden shapes formerly used in the development of prototypes. However, many factories, especially in Japan, remain wedded to the classic process: a rough and ready wooden frame covered in synthetic clay, which is then sculpted by hand using a whole range of tools and special scrapers. The small parts, the engine with its fins and nooks and crannies, the exhaust pipes and silencers and various plates are now often made from laser-cut resin, but until about 10 years ago these parts were all in wood, using soft types such as poplar.

●●●● **1925 Hoco 125** DKW, two-stroke, single-cylinder, air-cooled engine – 142cc (55 x 60mm) – 2.5hp at 3000rpm – Piston-port induction – Mixture lubrication - Magneto ignition – Belt transmission – Frame from two ash beams – Pendular front suspension on leaf springs – Rear shoe brake – 2.25 x 26in tyres – 60kg – 60kph.

A rough mock-up of the FJ 1100 that was to appear at the 1984 Paris Show. Crude wooden shapes were used as a base on which clay was applied to create the body shape.

The completed mock-up of the FJ 1100 (still designated FX!) just awaits painting before its final showing. The engine and small parts are all made from wood, even the rear-view mirrors and chain casing!

A cabinetmaker's joy displayed at the Sammy Miller Museum in Hampshire: an all-wood replica of a 1926 Royal Enfield.

Time to spare? Then do what this Italian sculptor did and build a wooden motorbike around a lawnmower engine.

MOTORCYCLES BY MAIL ORDER (1914—1953)

Early days in France and the United States

Hirondelle SAINT MF ETIENNE

Soon to be off to the front in 1914, this soldier is sitting astride a 3hp Deronzière. Note the MF-branded special crankcase. (Jean Bourdache Archive)

Long before the internet, you could buy a motorcycle by mail order. France was one of the pioneers in the field with the *Manufacture d'Armes et de Cycles de Saint-Étienne*, familiarly known as 'La Manu'.

This sales method appeared around 1880 with Manufrance's first catalogue, the perusal of whose contents would occupy many a long winter's evening in the country. La Manu, on its way to becoming the world number one in mail order sales, offered a complete range of everyday items: clothes, accessories, guns and various tools and machines. Yet it was not the first mail order firm in France to offer motorbikes as, in 1905, a big Parisian dealer sold Griffon and other brands under its own name. The first motorbikes appeared in La Manu catalogue in 1912. These were the Lyon-made Deronzières simply repainted and rebadged, but in the 1930s, Manufrance became a builder in its own right with an Aubier-Dunne-engined 100cc bike, the start of a steadily increasing range that drew very much on that of another Lyon motorbike manufacturer, Ultima. Manu changed to Nervor (Armor) engines in 1948, then Ydral and Lavalette, while Bernardet scooters appeared in the catalogue bearing the 'Hirondelle' (Swallow) logo, used by Manufrance for all its two-wheelers.

If internet sales had developed sooner, Manufrance would probably have survived, but in the 1970s, it fell victim to the spread of big stores and improved transport, and disappeared, although followed by the rise of other mail order firms such as La Redoute.

Scooters from the three American giants

France was not unique in this field and the other country selling bikes by mail order was the United States, where scooters were very much in vogue from the late 1930s to the start of the 1960s. *Popular Mechanics* began the trend before the Second World War and things really took off in 1946 with the Doodle Bug scooters sold by Gambles Stores. The big names in American stores followed suit with Sears, Roebuck and Co. and Montgomery Ward, and the rather basic American-style scooters sold in their tens of thousands. Sears distributed The Cushman under the Allstate brand then, in 1953, the Vespa, renamed the Allstate Cruiser, while Montgomery Ward sold the Mitsubishi Silver Pigeon (a copy of the Lambretta SD) under the name of Riverside, followed by the Lambretta LI 125.

The Bernardet scooter featured in the *Manufacture de Saint-Étienne*'s 1955 catalogue, where it was renamed 'Hirondelle' (swallow). Here, stocks in Bernardet's Bagneux factory are waiting to be delivered to the *Manufacture de Saint-Étienne*.

1947; one of the first post-war Hirondelles, the model B with its Ultima two-stroke 121cc engine offered four selector-operated gears. Unfairly it was little known, as the specialist press concentrated on the more heavily advertised manufacturers, yet the Hirondelle was still a commercial success.

The 1952 Manufrance catalogue.

Produced from 1951 to 1957, the attractive Allstar De Luxe, sold by mail order by Sears, was the result of an appealing restyling of the 1949 Cushman Model 621. (Keith & Kim Weeks Collection; Dregni & Dregni)

A rival of Sears Roebuck and Montgomery Ward in the US mail-order business, Gambles Stores also entered the scooter market in 1946 with this basic little scooter powered by a Briggs & Stratton lawnmower-type engine. It sold in tens of thousands! (Keith & Kim Weeks Collection; Dregni & Dregni)

The Allstar Jetsweep. Star of the Sears range between 1957 and 1960. (Keith & Kim Weeks Collection; Dregni & Dregni)

TWO-WHEEL-DRIVE MOTORCYCLES

Rex-OEC (1924-1935): The beginnings

The motorcycle is by nature unstable and since its earliest days some engineers have dreamed of tackling this problem by adding a powered front wheel; a strange idea, but effective. Those few 2 x 2 motorbikes that have been built demonstrate the point: the 1935 Rex-OEC, the late 1980s Savard and the Yamaha WR that took part in the Paris–Dakar race in the early 2000s (the only 2 x 2, along with the American Rokon off-road bikes of the 1960s, never to be put on the market).

It can clearly be seen that this is not a parallelogram fork, but a telescopic type.
(Tekniska Museet-Stockholm)

Based on a 1930 FN M67, even the first Sotrmark had a telescopic fork with the transmission gear and universal joint unit above the wheel. There are just two chains on the front transmission and the gearbox output sprocket is simply divided.
(Tekniska Museet-Stockholm)

The 2 x 2 motorbike has never achieved quantity production, being hampered by the technical complexity of the arrangement and its considerable cost, among other problems, including an unusual and somewhat disconcerting driving technique.

It appears that the first 2 x 2 motorbike was built in 1924 by the English engineer, Bill Bradley, with the two powered wheels driven by chains, using a Raleigh as the basis. About 10 years later, in Sweden, Eunar Sotrmark developed the system, proclaiming that on slippery ground and for transmitting greater power, two wheels were better than one.

Four chains for two wheels

Eunar Sotrmark's story begins in the early 1930s with a first attempt based on a 1930 FN 500 M67. The method of driving the front wheel took up the principle established by Bill Bradley and improved it so as to incorporate front suspension. The system was rather tricky in that the upper chain had to maintain a constant tension. Sotrmark cleverly achieved this by replacing the traditional parallelogram fork with an 'upside-down' telescopic fork, with the plunger tubes at the bottom sliding into the upper tubes. Thus the

● ● ● ● Four-stroke, two-cylinder V engine – 1370cc (86 x 117mm) – 90hp – OHV – Two twin-float carburettors – Magneto ignition – Separate gearbox – Chain transmission to the rear wheel –Disengageable intermediate gearbox and transmission to the front wheel by three chains and universal shaft – Twin downtube cradle frame – Inverted telescopic front suspension, no rear suspension.

The 1,370cc Rex-OEC on show at the Stockholm Technical Museum. We are looking at the side with the front final-drive chain and a universal joint on the transverse shaft above the wheel. (Tekniska Museet-Stockholm)

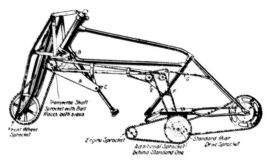

The drive train of the Felix with two driven wheels as designed in 1924 by Bill Bradley. The front suspension has gone and there are just two transmission chains at the front: the first forms an angle over the engine with a complex tensioning system. As an aside, the name 'Felix' chosen by Bradley comes from the cartoon *Felix the Cat*.

whole of the transmission attached to the long fork tubes moved with them like a swing arm and the two chains were consequently kept in constant tension. In 1934, Sotrmark improved the design by adopting not just two, but three chains to drive the front wheel. A second power take-off was mounted over the gearbox with a one-way clutch mechanism that acted as a differential.

1,370cc, 90hp, Four chains... and very small tyres

Sotrmark's extraordinary machine was developed from a very special OEC designed by the Swedish racer Berthold Ericsson, who had won race after race over the years. With the English OEC name being quite unknown in Sweden, Ericsson renamed his creation after his principal Swedish sponsor, Rex. The 750cc engine was replaced by a 1,000cc JAP that, later bored out to 1,370cc and run on methanol, delivered an astonishing output, for its time, of 90hp!

Ericsson contacted Eunar Sotrmark, by now well known for his experiments on motorbikes with two driven wheels, with the idea of adapting the system for the Rex-OEC. Ready by the spring of 1935, the bike easily won its first hill climb at Malmö on 22 April then, with a sidecar attached, it won the Swedish sidecar championships the same year. Sadly, it was not to last. The engine took on another life in a variety of motorbikes, ending up in a four-wheeled vehicle before being reassembled and restored to its historic form and put on display at Stockholm's Technical Museum.

The front of the upper transmission and its chain-tensioner. Note the superb twin-chamber carb. There's another one on the other side! (Tekniska Museet-Stockholm)

The other side of the Rex-OEC shows the complex arrangement of the transmission and the power take-off above the engine sprocket. It was thus possible to declutch the transmission or to let it slip to change gear easily. (Tekniska Museet-Stockholm)

The photo gives a good view of the engine layout and the controls above the long running board, as well as the two cranked brake pedals, which may be there to allow the driver to change position or to permit a passenger to participate in the process.

MGD [1947]
The French revolution

Apart from MGC, name another three-letter manufacturer also located in the department of the Isère and also beginning with MG... No? Well, you're missing a quite revolutionary machine.

Doubtless inspired by the 1939 Sévitame, the engineer Louis Debuit secretly began, before the end of the war, to design *the* ideal military motorcycle. It was built and developed between 1946 and 1947 in the Lyon workshops of MGD

(Merlin Gerin-Debuit), established in Grenoble in 1943. Less than two years to develop such a sophisticated engine was quite an achievement. All the more so in that Louis Debuit had improved the system by using front and rear shaft and universal joint transmission, and a gearbox with three road speeds and three low-ratio, all-terrain speeds.

Louis Debuit wanted to make as low-slung and compact a motorbike as possible. Simple! Ultima's Lyon factory was nearby and didn't baulk at more work on its books. The MGD's 500cc MG1-X40-type engine seemed to have taken its side-valve head from the Ultima X-series industrial engines (highly regarded and built up until the early 1950s). Fed by a tiny carburettor, it produced only 9hp at 3,000rpm. On the other hand, the engine block bore a very close resemblance to the Y-series motorcycle block from the late 1930s, and the whole unit was inclined forwards at about 70° to keep the bike's height as low as possible.

This novel and compact engine block also had the advantage of being linked to a three-speed gearbox with an auxiliary reducer that gave three high and three low ratios. A fan provided forced-air cooling and a pair of bevel gears at the end of the gearbox transmitted the power through two shafts, one forwards and one to the rear.

The highly sophisticated front transmission was via a shaft and bevel gears with a drum brake by the side of the latter. A double universal joint in the wheel hub controlled the steering via jointed rods. An idling wheel allowed the front wheel to turn more rapidly into bends or automatically applied power to the front wheel, distributing it 50–50, if the rear wheel began to skid.

Société dite :
**Société pour l'Exploitation
des Brevets M. G. D.**
(Société à Responsabilité Limitée)

Pl. unique

Fig. 1

Fig. 2

Fig. 3

Fig. 4

Fig. 5

Fig. 6

●●●● Ultima 499cc (84 x 90mm) engine (MG1-X40) – Side valves – Forced-air cooling – 9hp at 3,000rpm – Three-speed gearbox, double, coned clutch and speed reducer – Front shaft transmission, bevel gears with free wheel; shaft and bevel gears to the rear – Front hub steering with twin cardan shaft – Chassis from two light-alloy spars – Bodywork in aluminium sheet – Swing front suspension bearing on leaf springs – Light-alloy wheels and 500 x 15in tyres – Front and rear drum brakes, 162mm dia. – Wheelbase 1,200mm – Ground clearance 200mm – 155kg – 80km/h (50mph).

Fig. 1: Very low slung thanks to its inclined engine, the MGD even shows a passenger seat and backrests!

Fig. 2: This bird's-eye view shows the layout of the two transmission shafts and the reduction gear box, on the right-hand side of the engine. According to the patents, it should have been possible to change gear without declutching, but it is not known whether this refinement was adopted on the machine that was built.

Figs 3 and 5: A double universal shaft permitted U-turns on narrow, secondary roads, as was required in the Army specifications.

Fig. 4: Alloy wheel with six spokes, a big first.

Fig. 6: Cross section of the double universal joint system.

The first French light-alloy wheels

MGD also set off another revolution with its six-spoke light-alloy wheels with 500 x 15in tyres (like the Simca 5).

The cycle part and bodywork were reminiscent of the Majestic with a chassis consisting of two spars (apparently made from light alloy), with the front wheel axle supported by quarter elliptic springs. The all-enveloping bodywork was made from aluminium sheet, and the driver, sitting very low and well towards the front was provided with two long footrests; more like a military scooter than anything else. Thanks to the extensive use of light alloy, the MGD weighed just 155kg despite its heavy transmission.

It was also quite at home climbing 45° slopes and reaching 80kph (50mph), all while providing 200mm ground clearance and a very respectable turning circle of 2.75m, giving a U-turn of 5.5m.

Unfortunately, this fine machine failed to convince the armed forces and Louis Debuit returned to his original work of military arms manufacture, becoming well known in the late 1940s for his MGD PM9, a folding sub-machine gun weighing 2.5kg and firing 9mm Parabellums. He registered a number of patents up until the 1960s on engines, transmissions, weapons and a variety of electrical devices. Curiously, all his later patents on transmissions were filed in Canada – the country where the Rokon motorcycle with two powered wheels had its greatest success!

Wearing his clogs, Louis Debuit shows off his creation in 1947. (Louis Ballu)

Above all practical, the Rokon was in production for a good 20 years with few changes. (Jean-Michel Horvat Collection)

The notion of the two-wheel-drive motorcycle did not reappear until the late 1950s, and this time it was in the United States where a small team of enthusiasts launched the most novel of the utility bikes: the Rokon.

A two-wheeled tractor more than a motorbike, the Rokon was aimed at lumbermen and similar workers. In some respects very rustic, the machine was powered by a small West Bend, later Chrysler, engine linked to a hydraulic torque converter and a clutchless, three-speed gearbox. A transmission shaft in the big upper tube of the frame transmitted power to a gearbox and to a universal joint over the front wheel, which was then chain driven. The rear transmission was conventional. The aviation-type carburettor functioned regardless of its position.

The Rokon looked huge, yet weighed only 87.5kg dry, a marvel of lightness. It could move between 8 and 40km/h (5 and 25mph), clear serious obstacles thanks to its fat, low-pressure tyres and climb 60° slopes. Designed to cope with the most hostile environments, it had aluminium wheels that could also serve as reserve fuel or water tanks, or, if empty, to aid with flotation, should it find itself in excessively boggy territory! Virtually indestructible, the Rokon was made (in limited numbers) over a period of nearly 30 years without any major modifications.

●●●● **1964 Rokon**

Two-stroke, single-cylinder, air-cooled engine – 134cc – 8.5hp at 8000rpm – Flywheel magneto – Mixture lubrication – Hydraulic converter and three-speed gearbox operated by a lever on the left-hand side – Transmission by shaft, constant-velocity universal shaft and chains – Double-cradle frame – No suspension – Low-pressure 6.70 x 15in tyres – 17-litre water or petrol reserve tank in the wheels – 38cm ground clearance – 10-litre tank – 87kg – 40kph.

One of the last versions of the Trail-Breaker being demonstrated at the 1993 Coupes Moto Légende at Montlhéry.

Rokon [1960] The cowboys' 2 x 2

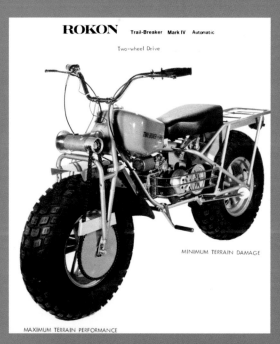

ROKON Trail-Breaker Mark IV Automatic

Two-wheel Drive

MINIMUM TERRAIN DAMAGE

MAXIMUM TERRAIN PERFORMANCE

With its 134cc, 9hp lawnmower engine it could reach a maximum of 40kph and climb a 60° slope.

A Savard built from a Yamaha TT 600 is given a private test by Yamaha Motor France's boss, Jean-Claude Olivier, proving in passing that the 2 x 2 could handle a skid without using opposite lock.

Savard [1987-1990] A French relaunch of the idea

Patrick and Franck Savard explain their system before the test.

By the 1980s, technological progress would finally allow the construction of light and efficient 2 x 2s. Sadly, it was too late: regulations hampered all innovation, drivers were unwilling to adapt their driving techniques and private initiatives would fail to get their projects into production, through lack of funds.

In France, a country with a predilection for novel and unusual ideas, the Savard brothers would, between 1987 and 1990, bring up to date and refine all the 2 x 2 motorcycle technology to the point where little more would have been needed to get their project into production. Franck Savard had started as an engineer involved in the development of the Elf 3, for which he came up with plans for front swing suspension with hub steering. Supported by Anvar, the national agency that distributed funds to the most promising projects, the Savard twins, Patrick and Franck, built their first motorbike with two powered wheels in 1987, powered by a Kawasaki 500cc cross engine that first successfully turned a wheel in anger at the Brittany 24-hr Enduro the same year. This engine gave way the following year to a Husqvarna 500 then an air-cooled Yamaha YZ 500. In 1989, there was a new prototype, still based on a Husky, but this time with a 510cc four-stroke engine and driven by Philippe Vassard (coming 171st out of 1,200 at the Le Touquet beach race in 1989), followed by Franck Sinet who came sixth in the French Supermotard Championships that year. The twins then built a Savard-Yamaha 600 TT before getting into some hazy design project of which nothing was ever heard again. This was a great shame as, with very limited resources, the Savard brothers had been able to demonstrate the potential of their design for enduro. The basis was a very light frame structure with a deformable parallelogram front suspension and hub steering.

The power distribution was close to 50–50 with a three-chain front-wheel transmission based on the principle established in 1924 as described in the first part of this

The 1988 Savard with a Yamaha 600cc engine. Easily identifiable are the transmission arrangement with its three chains, the very effective and rigid front suspension with its collapsible parallelogram, and the upper arm serving as a chain casing.

story. The transmission had an idler-wheel system on the output shaft so that the front wheel was not engaged until the rear wheel started to turn faster. Fearsomely effective over soft ground, the 2 x 2 nevertheless disconcerted most of the top drivers who tried it, finding that they had to completely alter their driving techniques to adapt to it. The broad skid pattern was particularly unsettling, as both of the bike's wheels remained in line, skidding in unison without the need to turn into it!

Éric Valat: an extra shaft

In 1988, in the south of France, Éric Valat also put together a 2 x 2 with an interesting novelty: the front-wheel transmission consisting of a chain and shaft and universal joints with an angle drive over the wheel that was chain driven in the standard way. In 1990, Éric improved and simplified this arrangement using an XT 600 as a basis, in which a bevel drive was placed directly by the output-shaft gear and transmission was by shaft and universal joints over the wheel.

David Watts: such an eccentric idea has to be British

France has no monopoly over novel ideas! To prove it, David Watts, of Northampton, built different prototypes based firstly on the Maico 400 in 1987, then on the Yamaha XT and TT 600 in 1988 and 1989, respectively. In classic style, like the 1936 Rex, the transmission was via three successive chains. The first ended in an angle drive and universal joint under the lower T of the retained original fork. The other two chains were laid out in scissor configuration and pivoted on a central gear so as to maintain a constant tension during movement of the telescopic fork. To add a (barely necessary!) touch of individuality to his second prototype, David Watts mounted the front disc brake on the end of the intermediate gear's pivot pin below the steering column. His final endeavour in 1989 used a Yamaha as its basis.

The 1988 Savard 2 x 2 with a Husqvarna engine.

David Watts's late-1989 British contribution: a disc brake on the front-wheel transmission. Not sure how well that worked!

Éric Valat in 1990 on his 2 x 2 with its simplified transmission using one shaft and chain.

The Suxuki XF5, seen here at the 1991 Tokyo Show, has a size advantage over other two-wheel-drive motorbikes: nothing wrong with its appearance.

The idea of two-wheel-drive motorcycles was in the air, and in the late 1980s it was the turn of the big players to try their hand at this new technology.

At the 1991 Tokyo Show, three of the big manufacturers demonstrated that they were involved in intensive research into the subject. Honda and Suzuki displayed several prototypes using this technology in various guises, and Yamaha was actually on the verge of commercialising theirs. Suzuki's first prototype two-wheel-drive motorbike was the Nuda, which had appeared at the 1987 Tokyo Show, even though it was probably little more than a styling exercise. On the other hand, the XF425 Ugly Duck and the XF5 displayed at the 1991 Tokyo Show appeared to be fully functional and virtually ready for production. In any event, it was Suzuki who were most advanced with their prototype development.

An 'Ugly Duckling' for the Americans

The Ugly Duck was aptly named, though far from being truly ugly, it actually possessed a certain appeal. This odd little machine seemed to have come straight from a cartoon, and this was not a matter of chance. The Japanese manufacturers were relying on the ease of handling afforded by the two-wheel drive to make a serious appeal to a non-specialist clientele and in particular to Americans partial to family-friendly leisure vehicles. In the minds of its designers, the Ugly Duck might perhaps have replaced the all-terrain three wheelers that had recently been withdrawn from sale for safety reasons after having been bought at the rate of 500,000 a year up to 1985.

On the Ugly Duck, in common with the XF4 Lander prototype also displayed by Suzuki at the same show, the transmission was continuous to both wheels (unlike on the XF5, which had an automatic clutch for the front wheel that took power off when adhesion was sufficient). An angle drive at the gearbox exit drove a kind of electronically controlled differential clutch, and a succession of three chains trans-

Suzuki, Honda, Yamaha (1991-2006) Japan gets involved

mitted the power to the front wheel. The gearbox was automatic, so as to make driving as simple as possible, and a large double seat emphasised its leisure credentials.

Suzuki XF5: a step forward without frightening off customers

The XF5 is more interesting, as its fairly conventional looks would make it more acceptable to potential customers. The telescopic front fork gives it the appearance of a traditional enduro bike. In fact, only the right leg of the fork acts as a suspension unit. The other leg is attached to the frame by means of a swing arm and houses a transmission shaft driven by a cumbersome train of three chains from the engine's output shaft. As on most modern 2WD bikes, a one-way clutch ensures that the drive is biased to the rear wheel.

One might question the weight penalty thus imposed, much of it unsprung. Yet experience so far has been promising and, as it is aimed at popularising the format among the sceptics, it seems worth watching on those grounds alone.

The engine is a standard two-stroke, 195cc with liquid cooling and a six-speed gearbox. It has 18-inch wheels.

Yamaha: pragmatism

Receptive to new technology, Yamaha showed interest in two-wheel drive as early as 1985. 'It has always been out of the question to use a mechanical transmission on the front wheel, as any locking would have catastrophic consequences,' commented an engineer at the release of the final version of the 2Trac in 2002. Öhlins, then 100% controlled by Yamaha, developed the system from 1985: the output-shaft gear drove a hydraulic pump via a short chain in an oil bath and was linked by two pipes to a tiny hydraulic motor housed in the front wheel. It was designed so that the more the rear wheel slipped, the more power was taken by the front wheel (up to a maximum of 20kW). In normal use, a very low level of power applied to the front wheel (about 10%) was sufficient to stabilise the bike on soft ground. On the TT600, the first bike so equipped, the device added just 10kg to the weight and used only 10% of the total power. In 2004, Yamaha and Öhlins adapted the system to the WR450, a machine that was to prove its effectiveness in the Paris–Dakar race, among others. This superb machine has the proud achievement of being the only two-wheel-drive motorcycle to be put into mass production by a major manufacturer, yet between 2004 and 2006, it would sell fewer than 100 machines.

The highly compact hydraulic motor developed by Öhlins is here positioned in the front hub of a TT 600. The one used on the WRF 450 2Trac is even smaller!

The Yamaha WRF 450 2Trac in action at the Shamrock Rally in 2002. Note that despite the skid, the driver has no need to counter-steer.

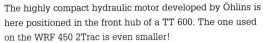

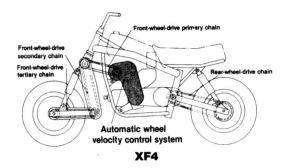

The complex transmission arrangement of the Suzuki XF4 with four chains for the front wheel.

Suzuki's 1991 XF4 would certainly not have gone unnoticed in the street!

The Honda Mantis: a very attractive praying mantis, though it's not known whether it really worked.

Honda Mantis: the leisure bike of the future

Though doubtless more effective in the hands of an expert, the two-wheel drive bike has largely been presented as a machine that is easier for beginners to handle, and Honda was well aware of this when it unveiled the Mantis at the 1991 Tokyo Show, an unusual, futurist bike that may be a forerunner of the leisure bike of tomorrow.

Unlike other bikes using chains and transmission shafts, Honda took a step towards the future by developing a fully automatic, electronically controlled transmission system for the Mantis. In doing this, Honda had not taken the easy route:

while much used in industrial applications, hydraulic transmission is difficult to adapt to a light vehicle where power loss has to be minimised and where small-diameter pipes have to allow rapid circulation of hydraulic fluid at very high pressures to power the motors on the 21-inch wheels.

Also noteworthy on this engineer's dream is a manual adjustment of the front/rear transmission ratio, a rear-transmission joint in carbon fibre, a single-leg parallelogram front suspension and a button on the handlebars for adjusting the level of damping.

THREE-SEATER MOTORCYCLES (1924-1939)

The most widespread Böhmerland, the St Gotthard type of 1927, with a dual seat plus a pillion. Unlike the Moto Maître, its road-holding was entirely sober. It was most frequently used with a sidecar.

Motorcycles are most often used by a single person, sometimes with a pillion rider and occasionally with a third wheel and a sidecar. A motorcycle with three seats, one behind the other, remains an exception. Until congestion on our urban roads brings the three-seater motorcycle back into fashion, let's take a little look back at the only two models that have attempted this risky enterprise: the Czech Böhmerland and the French Moto Maître.

●●●● **Böhmerland 600** Four-stroke, single cylinder, air-cooled – 603cc (80 x 120mm) – 20hp at 3,500rpm – Pushrod valve operation, exposed rockers – Magneto ignition – Separate three-speed manual gearbox – Double-cradle frame in two- and three-seater versions – Leading-link front suspension, friction dampers – 19in light-alloy wheels – 180kg – 120km/h (75mph) without sidecar.

From the early 20th century, Czechoslovakia was at the forefront of technological advances, thanks to its often highly innovative output in the motorcycle field: four cylinders and chain transmission from Laurin-Klement (later to become Skoda) in 1905, the first production double overhead camshaft (39 years before Honda) with the 1927 BD-Praga, alloy wheels in 1923 (53 years before Yamaha), electric starter in 1932 and so on. Even after the Second World War and despite being behind the Iron Curtain, the country succeeded in maintaining a substantial output that would not finally be strangled by Soviet 'planning' until the late 1950s.

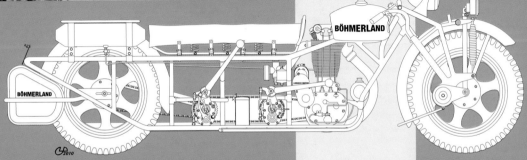

The Böhmerland 600cc three-seater, a 1937 prototype for the Army, with two Hurth (licensed from Sturmey Archer) coupled gearboxes. (Drawing by Yves Campion)

The classic Moto Maître is unusually elongated. Those who have test-ridden it come away awestruck! (Didier Ganneau)

An exceptionally long double-cradle frame

About 3,000 Böhmerland bikes ('Bohemia' in German) were built between 1923 and 1939 by Albin Liebisch, whose signature is visible on the engine. While the latter was very much a standard item, it was quite a different matter with the unusually long, heavily braced frame, which was available as a single-seater (over 140km/h [87mph]), a two-seater with an optional pillion seat and in 1937 a three-seater with two linked gearboxes was planned (by Hurth under licence from Sturmey Archer)! The driving position was fairly low, right up against the engine (with a rise in the saddle to avoid getting caught by the exposed rocker arms!), while there were two cylindrical fuel tanks beneath the luggage carrier. A large boot could be fitted right at the back. Using a similar frame, Böhmerland also built a two-stroke, 350cc, Liebisch-engined bike. Though sales ended in 1939, a final prototype, very much in the house style, appeared in 1952, with streamlining, a very long saddle about 50cm from ground level and a 198cc Zündapp engine.

60 Maîtres in 11 years

Eugène Maître, the workshop manager at Schneider Automobiles in Besançon, built his first motorcycle at the end of 1928. He then worked on his own account selling bikes and struggled along until 1938 having built and sold, with some difficulty, about 60 of them. Of conventional design, they had Chaise 500 SOHC, LMP and Moser engines plus, apparently, four examples powered by JAP 1,000cc transverse V engines and six others with a four-cylinder Train engine.

More than just an assembler of bikes, Eugène Maître built his own frames and forks and used the best accessories available for the other elements. Apart from his standard versions, Eugène also applied himself to multi-seat models, including a three-seater version that was virtually impossible to drive.

The double frame, without any rear suspension, was greatly lengthened, but with no other improvements than a vague shroud over the two rear triangles. Manoeuvrability and stability were not of the best, the turning circle was excessive and the frame's lack of rigidity allied to the standard front geometry — with a low fork rake — and the lengthy wheelbase caused constant and unsettling steering problems.

●●●● 1932 Moto Maître 500 three-seater

Single-cylinder, four-stroke, Chaise engine/gearbox unit — 499cc (85 x 88mm) — 16hp at 3,800rpm — Shaft-driven SOHC — Multi-disc wet clutch — Geared primary transmission, secondary by chain with an intermediate tensioner — Three-speed gearbox with direct lever change — Brazed double-cradle frame — Maître Druid-type parallelogram front fork — Drum brakes — 19in wheels — 14-litre tank — 170kg.

A Czech Böhmerland, in 1923.
(Prague Museum Archive)

In 1936, *La Moto* couldn't stop talking about the qualities of this revolutionary motorbike, which at that time was called simply the CP.

The CP Roléo was neither the best known nor the most prolific French brand, but it perfectly exemplifies the trends of its time, with its pressed-steel frame. And its racing pedigree is impressive!

Established in 1897 by Léon Rollet, the eponymous Parisian firm turned to motorcycle building in 1926 with a novel frame design in 'pressed-steel sheet totally triangular', as the publicity described it. The frame was actually a product of Couégnas et Piault (known under the abbreviation CP) and would be used in all the CP Roléo models for a period of seven years, before the company ceased production of motorbikes in 1932 as a result of the high cost of these frames. As simple as it was effective, this frame consisted of a 2mm sheet-metal box housing the fuel tank (12 or 14 litres, depending on the model) linking the steering column to the rear axle in a direct line. Front and rear struts, also in pressed-steel sheet, completed the triangulation and carried the engine and gearbox. The Druid-type fork, with its springs mounted behind the legs, was made from the same material. It created a pleasing overall appearance and it's clear from the drawings that it must have been very rigid, perhaps a little too much so with its ancient fork as the only means of suspension.

The remarkable Harrissard engine

The first, 1926-built bike won victory after victory: at the Armistice Cup, the Côtes d'Argenteuil and Château-Thierry races, then at the Bol d'Or, where it came first in the 350cc category on the St-Germain-en-Laye circuit, covering 1,459km (907 miles) at an average of 61km/h (38mph), with, of course, just a single driver, as was the practice at the time. It then took first place in 1926 in the well-known Paris–Les Pyrénées–Paris rally in which the three motorbikes entered

SHEET-METAL MOTORCYCLES

CP Roléo (1925-1932) A frame and three Bol d'Or

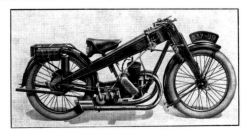

Taken from *La Moto* in 1926, this view of the Harrissard two-cylinder engine shows the unusual arrangement of the carburettor, which was very exposed in a crash.

Harrissard advert following the 1926 Bol d'Or, when the CP Roléo won joint first place in the Paris–Nice.

... And following the Paris–Les Pyrénées–Paris race.

completed the course with no significant problems, and it finished the year in fine style by completing the Grand Prix de France at an average speed of 88.7km/h (55mph). The brilliant CP was powered by the remarkable Harrissard engine, a 350cc, two-stroke, two-cylinder engine that foreshadowed all the modern two-stroke twins and produced between 10 and 12hp at 4,000rpm. It was made by putting together two of the brand's 175cc engines. Each one retained half an engine crankcase vertically split, and these two half casings were attached to a central casing, this one with a horizontal gasket. The connecting rod assembly, set to 180°, ran in two ball-bearing units and a central plain bearing. The production version had cast-iron cylinders, but on the racing version they were aluminium. This very modern engine was fed by a single carburettor, curiously mounted on the right-hand side facing forwards and was thus vulnerable in the event of a crash. A pipe below the exhaust ports linked the inlet ports of the two cylinders. On the 350 racing CP, the Harrissard engine had a three-speed Staub gearbox and there were drum brakes front and rear. Harrissard also advertised single-cylinder 125 and 175cc as well as twin 250, 350 and 500cc engines.

From this somewhat limited output, it appears that only a 350cc racing-version engine has survived (with bore and stroke of 59 x 64mm, compared with 60 x 60mm on the touring version) and it is quite possible that the touring versions existed only on paper. The few rare examples that have left their mark on history are, at any rate, racing versions: one engine in a Durandal, at least three 350cc engines in the Paris–Les Pyrénées–Paris CP Roléos, and one in the Villard three-wheel sidecar bike that won the 1926 Bol d'Or. In the 1927 Bol d'Or, the three CP Roléos entered were powered by two-cylinder Harrissards of 250, 350 and 500cc, proof that three-cylinder versions must have existed. The three bikes finished the race, which won the Constructors' Cup for CP Roléo, but this time there was no one on the podium.

Nothing more was heard of Harrissard engines after 1928, but CP Roléo, keeping faith with two-stroke engines for racing, once again won the Bol d'Or at Saint-Germain-en-Laye in 1928, covering 1,446km (899 miles) at an average of 60.3kph, with an equally novel engine, a single-cylinder 350cc Pauvert with a rotary valve induction.

The four-stroke era
Fortified by its early racing success, CP Roléo extended its range in 1927, offering two-stroke, single-cylinder 175s and 250s, a Pauvert two-stroke 350 and four-stroke 250, 350 and 500 LMP engines. CP Roléo were the joint winners of the 1928 Paris–Nice with a rocker-valve LMP 350, Renaud coming first in the two-stroke 350 category with a Pauvert-engined CP Roléo. It has to be said that with the rules then in force, the majority of the competitors were joint winners in one category or other! By the October 1928 Paris Show, the two-stroke machines had disappeared from the catalogue and CP Roléo was using new Staub engines in its whole range. This compact unit brought the best of both worlds by marrying a Staub-gearbox-fitted block to a head, built under licence from the English firm of Jap, with matching dimensions. This provided a more modern unit than most available in England and included twin-circuit pressure lubrication and enclosed valves. As was the fashion at the time, there were twin exhaust outlets and the gearbox could be taken out without removing the engine. Note in passing that the three gears were reversed, with first at the rear, and that the ignition advance control was operated by a twist grip on the left side of the handlebar, as on American bikes. CP Roléo continued to enter its bikes for the big races and won two brilliant victories for the last time in 1929, including a second Bol d'Or for Renaud on a CP Roléo with a 250cc Staub-JAP engine that broke all records, covering 1,521km (945 miles) at an average of 63.4km/h (39.4mph).

A very rare CP Roléo with a Pauvert engine.

No place on the podium in the 1927 Bol, but the three Harrissard-engined CP Roléos, each with different cylinder capacities, did manage to finish. The drawing shows the twin's design with its induction tract ahead of the cylinders, beneath the bulbous exhaust outlets, and its four engine casings: two with horizontal gaskets in the middle and two vertical casings on the sides.

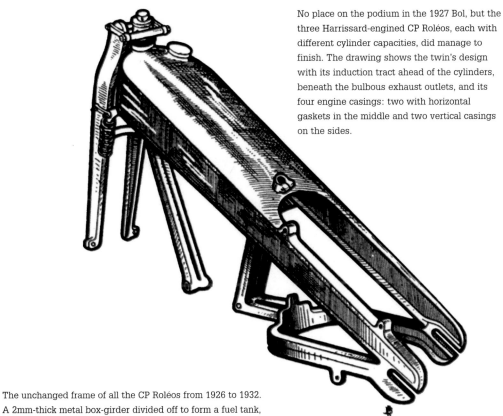

The unchanged frame of all the CP Roléos from 1926 to 1932. A 2mm-thick metal box-girder divided off to form a fuel tank, with a few metal struts to hold the engine and join it to the gearbox at the rear of the frame. (Drawing from *La Moto*)

One of the rare surviving examples with a 1929 Staub-JAP 350 engine, during a rally.

The frame was significantly simplified when the Staub-JAP engine was adopted, as it was no longer required to support a separate gearbox.

The CP Roléo with a LMP engine on show at the Amnéville Museum.

Robert Sexé (behind) on his Gillet 500 Supersport, during his tour of Europe in 1928, meets another long-distance traveller on a CP Roléo 500 LMP, at Hermanstadt in Romania.

Escol (1925-1938)
A case apart

It was all Jules's fault. The father of the Escol family, an engineer with the State Coal Board, passed on his love of mechanical things to his eldest sons, Félix and Maurice.

Born respectively in 1900 and 1904, the Escol boys developed a taste for motorcycling as they tried out everything the American and European armies had left behind as surplus after the First World War. Having wrecked a few of them on the potholed roads of the time, they came up with something of a revolution at the 1920 Brussels Show: the Spring, a curious concoction with a transverse V engine block and front and rear suspension with a compensation device that took account of the bike's loading. Unfortunately, while the Spring was comfortable, it was fragile. So in 1922, Félix and Maurice decided to realise an old dream and make their own bike that would be financed by their father, Jules. Three years later it was ready, and included, without any consideration of the cost, all the features the two brothers had dreamt of.

The Super-Moto, every feature, regardless of price

It's true that its appearance was not intended to be refined, but technically it was so well thought out that the two brothers covered over 200,000km on it without any significant problems. The engine-transmission unit was fixed to a removable false chassis in the huge pressed-steel frame, which was one of the first of its kind. The power unit, gearbox and electrics were thus readily accessible. With the Anzani engine they used having been designed for small cars or light planes, no motorcycle gearbox would have coped with its power. The brothers therefore developed their own gearbox with the unusual feature of separate lubrication for each element according to the load.

Unique, the huge Super-Moto gives a final demonstration in 1972 with Félix, Maurice and Jules Escol, who had covered over 200,000km on it. On this evidence, should the Super-Moto now be filed under three-seaters?
(Patrick Escol Archive)

Comfort comes first thanks to a very sophisticated suspension. (Patrick Escol Archive)

The best technology of its period and one of the first with a pressed-metal frame. (Patrick Escol Archive)

The robust Anzani 1,000cc engine coupled to a home-built transmission.

Unparalleled roadholding and comfort

Low and very long, the Escol had exemplary roadholding, aided by effective front and rear suspension and big tyres. It could almost do a U-turn on the spot: the driver would lean it over on one footboard and turn it 180°. Local lore claimed that a glass of beer placed on the parcel carrier would remain upright while going over a level crossing!

Too expensive for you, I'm afraid

Unfortunately, had it been put into production, this 'châtelettaine', as it was sometimes known, after the Châtelet workshops near Charleroi where it was built, would have cost around 30,000 Belgian francs, a completely unaffordable price when a pushrod OHV 500FN cost only 7,750 Belgian francs at that time. After moving on to car building without getting to the commercialisation stage, the Escols decided in 1929 to launch their own brand of

motorcycle by reusing, on a reduced scale, the main principles of their Super-Moto: maximum protection for the bike and its driver and ease of maintenance. It took just 32 seconds to remove the rear mudguard, 33 seconds for the rear wheel and 76 to put them both back. A range of three models was displayed at the 1932 Brussels Show: two 500cc models and a 600, all with JAP engines and Burman gearboxes. The range was added to shortly after with lighter and less costly models with Villiers two-stroke engines of 200 and 250cc, followed in 1937 by a 350cc with four foot-pedal-operated gears.

The frame adopted the same pattern, the fork, which lost its compensator springs, retained just one middle spring and the engine-gearbox unit was still mounted on a false chassis.

It was a craftsman's world: Escol's 10 or so workers built only 270 motorbikes between 1932 and 1939, with the apotheosis of the final year being a 680cc, Jap V-twin, intended to be matched with a sidecar.

●●●● 1926 Escol Super-Moto

Anzani twin-cylinder, air-cooled, transverse-V engine – 987cc (85 x 87mm) – Side valves – Magneto ignition – Escol gearbox with three speeds and reverse – Multi-disc clutch – Chain transmission – Frame/body with a false chassis for the engine – Trailing-link front suspension with three extension springs and two compensator springs; rear swing suspension with leaf springs and friction dampers – Rear band brake – 710 x 90 or 715 x 115 solid-disc wheels – Length 2.75m – 380kg – 115km/h (70mph).

The Escol firm also offered a sidecar in 1933, built entirely in their workshops. (Yves Campion Archive)

The zenith of this style, with its extraordinary purity of line, on a 1933 500cc. (Patrick Escol Archive)

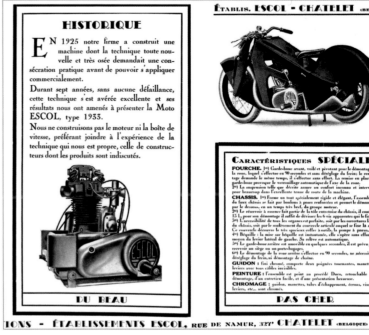

A leaflet for the 1933 range. (Yves Campion Archive)

An impressive meeting of Escol enthusiasts at the café du Châtelet in 1938. (Patrick Escol Archive)

The Escol stand at the Brussels Salon in late 1932. (Patrick Escol Archive)

The final generation of Escol: a 1937 350cc with a Villiers engine. (Jean Lecoq Collection)

At the 1927 Bol d'Or, run for the first time at Fontainebleau, this amazing 600cc New Motorcycle with a Peuple sidecar and driven by Messager, finished first (and was the only one placed!) in its category, covering the twenty-four hours at an average of 41kph. The machine is seen here at the start of the Paris–Les Pyrénées–Paris race, which it failed to finish because of an accident. Note the air-intake scoops for the cooling system, the exhaust outlet at the rear, and the petrol bottle on the luggage rack. The spectators sport an interesting variety of footwear.

New Motorcycle [1926-1929]

In the early 1920s, a few clever inventors were thinking that rolling and folding sheets of metal would be much more effective and economical than bending and welding tubes. A fair point!

Sheet-metal frames were flourishing throughout Europe from the early 1920s, in Germany, Belgium and France, with, in the latter, Janoir, Durandal and CP Roléo. This fashion would grow into its golden age in the 1930s with fairly large production runs making the enormous cost of the cutting and pressing machines more economically viable. Paradoxically, it was with economy in mind that Georges Roy, a self-taught engineer and motorcycle enthusiast, set about constructing a motorbike in sheet metal! Long, low and slender, his New Motorcycle, under development since 1923, and on display at the Paris Show in late 1926, would establish itself as one of the finest French touring bikes of the period.

Simple and effective: the motorbike on a roll

Built in the Orléans factory and assembled and painted in the Châtenay-Malabry workshops in the Paris suburbs, the New Motorcycle stood out for its simple and effective as well as economical construction. Builder Georges Roy's genius lay in using pressed-steel technology while minimising the cost of investment in machine presses. It would perhaps be more accurate to speak of a rolled steel frame rather than pressed. The shape was cut out in thick sheet then shaped in a press. Light tools were then used to fold over the sides, and the chassis/body thus shaped, extending right back to the rear axle, was riveted together

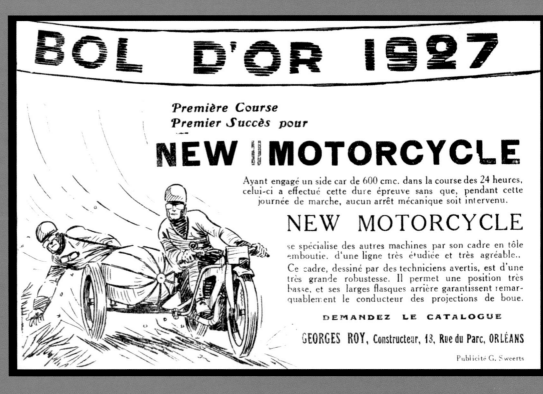

BOL D'OR 1927

Première Course
Premier Succès pour

NEW ‖ MOTORCYCLE

Ayant engagé un side car de 600 cmc. dans la course des 24 heures, celui-ci a effectué cette dure épreuve sans que, pendant cette journée de marche, aucun arrêt mécanique soit intervenu.

NEW MOTORCYCLE

se spécialise des autres machines par son cadre en tôle emboutie, d'une ligne très étudiée et très agréable. Ce cadre, dessiné par des techniciens avertis, est d'une très grande robustesse. Il permet une position très basse, et ses larges flasques arrière garantissent remarquablement le conducteur des projections de boue.

DEMANDEZ LE CATALOGUE

GEORGES ROY, Constructeur, 13, Rue du Parc, ORLÉANS

Publicité G. Sweerts

The New Motorcycle stand at the Paris Show, held in the Grand Palais in 1928. All the models on show are fitted with Chaise engines. A blank for the pressed-sheet frame is being used as a sign.

with a few internal strengtheners. The rear mudguard was fixed to this assembly, along with a forged-steel steering column. This simplest of cycle frames could take whichever of the principal engines available was requested: the modest two-stroke 175, 250 and 350cc Train engines, the four-stroke 350cc Anzani with side valves, or a four-stroke JAP or Zurcher – all with a Picard gearbox – or a Chaise engine block that was used on the last models.

The 1926 Salon catalogue offered no fewer than 12 models and the January 1929 catalogue, seven, ranging from the short-lived, utility 175cc Train, to the OHV, or SV 350 and 500cc Jap with Standard, Super-Confort, Sport, Super-Touriste and Super-Sport versions. A fine range, but as even Georges Roy himself admitted, few of these versions actually went on sale and the great majority of New Motorcycles would be powered by Chaise engines. It was a difficult start, but the sporting success quickly achieved (at the 1927 Bol d'Or with a sidecar, the winter 1928 Six Days Trial, the Paris–Nice etc) would bring it to public attention and the New Motorcycle would eventually meet with deserved success in its short career from 1927 to the end of 1929, including in the export market, from Germany to Czechoslovakia.

For Georges Roy, the New Motorcycle was just a first step. Buoyed by his success, he pursued his dream to make the ideal Grand Touring bike, the New Motor-Car, which he unveiled in March 1929, later selling it as the Majestic. Much more sophisticated and a bit disconcerting with its steering hub, and also more expensive, the splendid Majestic would frighten off many customers and it is estimated that only about 220 were produced between 1929 and 1934. It's always risky to be too far ahead of one's time, but Georges Roy's New Motorcycle and Majestic creations were among the most significant in the history of the French motorcycle.

TYPES 350 & 500 CM3

500ccm

MONOBLOC GRAND-SPORT — Double échappement.

Touly·PARIS

This illustration of the 350 and 500cc model in the 1929 catalogue shows how the frames evolved: small openings on the pre-series, three side openings on the 1928 version (in colour on p. 88) and only two larger ones after the 1928 Salon.

●●●● Georges Roy: from knitting to the motorcycle

Born in 1888 in the Touraine, Georges Roy was apprenticed at the age of 12, after his school certificate. Four years later, he went up to Paris 'with just three francs in my pocket'. He then went to Mantes-la-Jolie where he built a small two-stroke engine. Becoming a turner following the First World War, he settled in Orléans where his career and fortune would be decided. Here, he

bought his first knitting machine and from that moment devoted his life to the machines, filing a number of patents that are still in use today. Motorbikes would be just a brief, six-year interlude 'between two jumpers', as he put it to me during an interview in 1973, but what an interlude!

After the brilliant New Motorcycles, built from 1926 until 1929, would come the revolutionary Majestics, whose manufacture would be handed over in 1930 to Delachanal company the builders of Dollar motorbikes.

The builder, Georges Roy, at the age of 38, poses before the 1926 Salon with the first New Motorcycle powered by a two-stroke Train 350. The subsequent versions had larger side openings in the frame.

This 1928 New Motorcycle is powered by a Chaise OHC engine. Appearing in 1927, these Chaise engines offered a whole generation of unexciting but modern and reliable engineering. The New Motorcycles used the 350 and 500 engines with SOHC driven by a shaft and bevel gear from 1927, followed by the rocker-valve versions in 1929.

The introductory page from the 1927 catalogue leaves no doubt that this is a revolution!

Unless specially ordered (with a 300-franc supplement!) the New Motorcycles were delivered in 'hunting blue' with a mahogany top to the tank body, but the splendid slender body gave rise to all sorts of fantasies, as shown by this entirely rubbed down version that made the cover of the *Petit Journal* on 24 March 1935. (Bernard Salvat Archive)

●●●● 1929 New Motorcycle Chaise (350) 500

Chaise four-stroke, single-cylinder, air-cooled engine – 500cc (82 x 90mm) – Shaft and bevel-gear drive SOHC – Mechanical-pump lubrication – Wet multidisc clutch – Manual three-speed gearbox – Chain transmission – Rolled sheet frame riveted on to transverse strengthening pieces – Parallelogram front suspension – 170mm-diameter drum brakes – 3.50 x 19in tyres, or optional Confort Bibendum balloon tyres – (145) 160kg – (105) 120km/h (75mph).

Georges Roy with his first creation, from 1916, a child's-type scooter with a four-stroke Dufaux engine. The transmission is direct to the front wheel, using the smallest possible sprocket: only seven teeth!

MOTORCYCLES WITH SKIS AND STUDDED TYRES (1925-1980)

A similar balance, the same pleasure of leaning into one bend after the other... motorcycling and skiing have a number of things in common. From that premise to combining the two is a bit of a leap, yet some makers have done it. Furthermore, the military don't shy from anything. From a strange hybridisation of the two activities would later come the highly successful skidoos.

The main problem with a two-wheeler is its lack of stability on slippery terrain. The problem has still not been resolved, despite all manner of engineers having applied themselves to the problem since the dawn of motorcycling.

The first solution: stopping the bike from skidding

In the early years of the century, accessory makers came up with a studded strip that was strapped to the tyres.

This device didn't do much for power output and didn't last well, but in 1933, Michelin invented the studded tyre for cars. This solution has never been well received in motorcycling circles, despite its effectiveness. I, myself, covered thousands of kilometres in the early 1970s with studded trail tyres and can assure you that they are perfect on icy roads.

Studded tyres are also used on the race track, but we're entering another world here, that of racing over ice using four-stroke, single-cylinder, methanol-fuelled bikes with 500 razor-sharp 75mm nails on each tyre, allowing bikes to lean at staggering angles. Begun around 1925 in Germany, and becoming popular in Russia and the Scandinavian countries, racing on ice has had its own world championship since 1966. In 1977, the first ice racing took place in Oklahoma, in the

The start of a winter rally in Sweden in 1929, showing an Indian equipped with side skis.

SVENSK MOTOR TIDNING

N:o 4
28 Febr.

OFFICIELLT ORGAN FÖR: KUNGL. AUTOMOBIL KLUBBEN, KUNG-
LIGA MOTORBÅT KLUBBEN OCH K. A. K:s LANDSFÖRBUND

1929
Årg. XXIV

Chefredaktör: Charlie Svenson | Telefoner: Namnanrop "AUTOMOBILKLUBBEN" | Verkst. direktör: Curt Svedelius

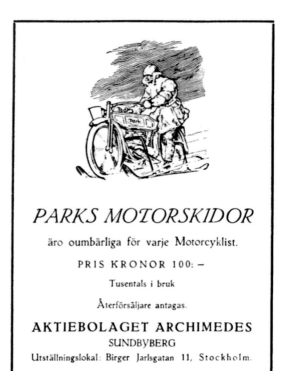

PARKS MOTORSKIDOR

äro oumbärliga för varje Motorcyklist.

PRIS KRONOR 100: —

Tusentals i bruk

Återförsäljare antagas.

AKTIEBOLAGET ARCHIMEDES
SUNDBYBERG
Utställningslokal: Birger Jarlsgatan 11, Stockholm.

A Swedish advertisement from the 1920s
for motorbike-adaptable skis.

A race on ice in Russia, 1929.

The supreme refinement offered in the 1930s by the great
German accessory-maker Framo: a pair of folding skis that
could double up as leg guards.

United States, after which American championships were
established in the sport.

Second solution: control the skid

If you're going to skid, you might as well try and control it
and it seems that the idea of combining the ski and the
studded wheel is as old as the motorbike itself. Indeed, in
Jean Bourdache's indispensable book *Motocyclette en
France de 1894 à 1914*, there is a period drawing of Daimler's
1885 motorcycle, the first petrol-engined two-wheeler,
fitted with a ski at the front, a studded tyre at the rear and
two sliders at the sides in place of the usual small wheels (all
licensed in 1885!). The vehicle might well have been
observed in action on a frozen lake somewhere near Herr
Doktor Daimler's workshops.

The idea took a while to catch on, as we have found no
further trace of a snowmobile until the late 1920s in a Swedish
newspaper article, dated 28 February 1929, devoted to a local
rally held in snowy conditions, in which the star, Richard
Svensson is riding an Indian fitted with skis at the side. It is
hardly surprising that this fitting would mainly have been
developed in the Nordic countries, where it was regularly used
on military motorcycles, civilians being more inclined to leave
the motorbike in the garage during the winter!

Patent for the Daimler with skis and studs, 1885. (Jean Bourdache Archive)

From ski bikes to skidoos

A pair of skis on a motorbike is fine, but better things can be done. Right at the start of the 1950s, there was a fashion for impossible scooter exploits. In 1952, the dare-devil Parisian, Georges Monneret, set out across the Channel on a Vespa attached to a boat hull, while over in the Alps, Jean Struder from Grenoble attacked the Col de Clemencière on a Vespa rather crudely fitted with double caterpillar tracks driven by friction off the rear wheel, with the front wheel attached to a ski. After this initial experience, Jean Struder went for the Col du Grand-Saint-Bernard on a very carefully prepared caterpillar Lambretta. Again, the front wheel was fitted with a ski, but the rear of the 1952 Lambretta had been completely modified. An articulated unit on the wheel added a second wheel at the rear of the scooter. Wooden drums on the wheels carried rubber caterpillar tracks and a V-belt transmitted the power to the second rear wheel. Familiar as we are with snowmobiles, the set-up seems unsurprising nowadays, but at the time it was quite revolutionary. I haven't delved into the matter of patents, but unless I am much mistaken, Struder would appear to be

the inventor of the single-track skidoo, as the Auto-Neige, invented in the winter of 1919–1920 then built and put on the market by Joseph-Armand Bombardier in 1937, has two skis at the front and two caterpillar tracks at the rear, and while the first 'snowmobile' – the 1959 skidoo, also by Bombardier at Valcourt in Canada – has only one rear caterpillar track, it retains two skis at the front.

The idea of a single-track snowmobile based around a motorbike was recently revived by 2Moto, an American accessory specialist based in Idaho that sells kits consisting of a front ski support and a rear chassis incorporating suspension and a caterpillar track that can be fitted to the main enduro and motocross bikes on the market.

A proper motorcycle with skis, designed at the request of the Finnish Army by Moto Guzzi in the mid-1930s. This little-known bird in the range, the Cigogna (stork), is a prototype derived from the Alce 500, lightened as much as possible by the extensive use of light alloys.

Fitted with a ski just for show, a militarised Testi 50 on show at the 1980 Bologna Salon. The idea didn't catch on with young Italians. By contrast, in the more northerly countries, military bikes would often have this feature.

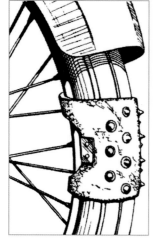

A studded strip to go over the tyre, from the late 1920s: *'Like octopus suckers, quick to attach, no wear, and silent...'*

The Zündapp is a standard model, but this clever Austrian luggage carrier from 1932 allows you to carry skis.

Das Motorrad auf Schlittenkufen

In dem Tiroler Wintersportparadies Kitzbühel erregte ein Motorradfahrer Aufsehen, der sein Fahrzeug mit Schlittenkufen versehen hatte und auf diese Weise trotz des schneereichen Winters auf den vereisten Straßen vorwärts kam.

With three wheels and two skis is a much safer way to tackle the 1930 Tyrol snow.

A Jawa type 889 ice-racing bike from 1962. Fuelled by methanol, the single-cylinder, 500cc machine develops around 50hp and weighs only 128kg.

Five hundred 75mm nails sharpened to a razor point for racing on ice.

●●●● **2.469m up and minus 18°C**

We may admire the innovative features and superb construction of this first, single-track snow scooter, yet we should not forget the sporting achievement involved in the ascent of the Great St Bernard Pass (2,469m) that Jean Struder himself describes in an article published at the time in *Science et Vie*: 'I chose the Great St Bernard Pass because it's one of the highest in Switzerland and there is more snow there. We had to assess the weather conditions, the avalanche risk, and find the best way across; the state of the snow varied considerably, in some places being very hard, in others blown or powdery. The avalanche crossings proved to be the most difficult and delicate passages. We had to clear a way across using a shovel in some places, and attach a rope to me, as the snow was giving way on very steep slopes across the mountainside. There was at that time no way from the road to the hospice [the motor-road built in 1905 is closed in winter and the tunnel that goes under the pass was not opened until 1964]. At the summit of the pass, the monks told me that more than 10m of snow had fallen that season and the temperature at 8am had been minus 18°C. I didn't once stop the engine for fear that the gearbox oil would freeze.'

Initial trials: Jean Struder's Vespa modified by Galtier attacks the Col de Clemencière, above Grenoble. (Photopress Grenoble)

Jean Struder's 1952 Lambretta, very carefully prepared and well equipped, sets out to conquer the Great St Bernard Pass. (Photopress Grenoble)

Even with a member of the ski patrol to clear the way of obstructions and with two skis on his feet, going uphill in the fresh snow doesn't look easy. (Photopress Grenoble)

Tired, Mr Struder? Or was this just to give us the opportunity to admire the caterpillar attachment? (Photopress Grenoble)

The Mercier caterpillar bike in its first, 1936, version, rather weakly powered by a single-cylinder JAP side-valve engine. The fork is quite different from the one that would be fitted to later versions and the front caterpillar unit is much less refined, but there is also one at the back! (Daniel Tille Archive)

Producing the all-terrain bike has always been a dream. After ski-bikes come bikes with caterpillar tracks... a story that begins, inevitably, with military examples and ends, more playfully, with the skidoo.

First a definition: what do we mean by a bike with caterpillar tracks? There are three schools:
● The single-tracked bike with a single caterpillar in place of each of the two wheels, or with one caterpillar plus one wheel or ski in the same alignment, such as in the case of the Mercier or the Le Haître;
● Double-tracked, or more often triple-tracked, where a pair of caterpillars takes the place of the rear wheel while the front wheel is retained, the first example of which was the René Gillet Chevreau that appeared in 1934, but did not get beyond the prototype stage, and the best-known model, the German Kettenkraftrad;
● Snowmobiles with a single, wide caterpillar at the rear and a pair of skis at the front.

Mercier: the front-caterpillar bike

The first single-track caterpillar bikes were, it seems, invented in the mid-1930s in response to a tender put out by the French Army (for which the well-known and much more effective Sévitame was also created). Thus the Mercier bikes appeared in 1936, followed by the Le Haître two years later.

The Mercier caterpillar bike was a pure single-tracked vehicle, in which, doubtless with the aim of lightening the steering (!), Mercier had placed both engine and caterpillar at the front. Well sheltered behind a huge screen made, not from Plexiglas, but armoured steel, the side-valve JAP engine transmitted its modest power to the front, steerable track via three successive chains. The caterpillar was steel with a

MOTORCYCLES WITH CATERPILLARS (1936-1945)
From caterpillar tracks to snowmobiles

Looking very smart in his plus-fours, the builder of the 1937 Mercier with its 350cc pushrod OHV JAP engine demonstrates that no obstacle will stop his improbable machine. (By the way, what happens when the caterpillar has cleared the rock or you meet an obstacle that throws you sideways?) (Daniel Tille Archive)

rubberised band. Remarkably, this curious machine conformed to the Army's weight specifications, being within 160kg (without the windscreen!). The driving caterpillar, swivelling around its central axis could tilt at 40° to clear obstacles. The feeble side-valve Jap was replaced in 1937 by an OHV 350cc Jap sport version putting out a respectable 11hp and matched with a separate three-speed gearbox (hand-operated by a lever at the front of the steering column!). The ultimate test came on 9 February 1937 at the Polygone de Vincennes, when the magnificent Mercier had to tackle slopes of 42° and 45°. Confident of the potential of this machine born of a somewhat utopian specification, the wise generals, never in any doubt, invited the Mercier back in 1939. This time, it failed on lack of power, even though it had climbed for 11m up a 45° slope and its intrepid drivers had touched 60km/h (37mph). (The current owner swears he would not attempt such an experience!)

Down but not out, Mercier went back to the drawing board, simplifying and strengthening the front caterpillar's support cradle and, above all, replacing the Jap with a 540cc, two-stroke, two-cylinder engine set at 180° that Aubier-Dunne had designed for the 'poux du ciel' (flying lice!), mini-aircraft that were so much in vogue in the pre-war years. Intended to be mounted upside down in an aircraft, the two-cylinder engine was here returned to the normal configuration and attached to the steering unit. Fed by a rotary inlet valve and provided with separate lubrication in addition to the mixture, it proudly put out 20hp at 4,000rpm. Unfortunately, the builders, perhaps having lost confidence in it or not wanting to face the possibility of a further rejection, did not show their new creation to the Army, who failed to call them back.

The builders pictured on two 1937 versions. Note the gear-change handles in front of the handlebars and the side covers on the caterpillars. (Daniel Tille Archive)

Exhibited at the Rétromobile Salon in 2008, this 1937 Mercier caterpillar bike boasts a cooling fan with a shapely duct feeding air to the cylinder head (and on to the driver sitting immediately behind!). The lack of side panels allows us to admire the superb cast-aluminium struts supporting the caterpillar. Either not strong enough or too costly, they would be ditched on the Aubier-Dunne-engined version. (In the background, is the 1937 OHV 350 version.)
(Daniel Tille Archive)

Mr J. Le Haître himself demonstrates the 'mono-caterpillar's' potential. Unfortunately, he was the only person to think it had any.

Le Haître: a built-in caterpillar

Already known for an odd motorbike displayed at the 1935 Lépine Contest, and whose sheet-metal upper bodywork lifted to give access to the engine, the engineer Le Haître revealed his caterpillar bike to the public at the May 1938 Paris Fair.

Why make anything complicated? Le Haître used just the caterpillar, which the driver straddled (with a saddle for protection). The rubber 'Kégresse' caterpillars (like those on a First World War tank), went right around the 500cc air-cooled Chaise engine and its accessories housed in an interior frame. The caterpillar was supported on five rollers, two upper ones, two lower and one at the front, which were moveable to maintain tension. So that's the caterpillar, but how did it move? Well, if I've understood this correctly, the leading roller turned, folding the caterpillar around it; on the other hand, the handlebars also controlled the small side wheels by lowering the one on the side into which one was turning. In short, the Le Haître, which weighed a good 414kg, was not a marvel of manoeuvrability and, like the Mercier, was rejected by the Vincennes examining committee, in contrast to the Sévitame, which while failing on its first attempt, brilliantly succeeded at the second.

The case of the Kettenkraftrad

The only really well-known caterpillar bike and the only one to be produced in numbers is the NSU-Opel HK 101, or Kettenkraftrad, designed and built by NSU and powered by a liquid-cooled, four-cylinder engine taken from an Opel Olympia. (According to German sources, 8,345 were turned out between 1941 and 1944, with perhaps more in 1945.)

It answered a reasonable-enough requirement, initially at any rate, to carry German soldiers across the snow on the Russian Front. Although designed for that purpose, the majority of them did not last long there.

Was it really a motorbike? Unlike the Mercier and Le Haître machines, the Kettenkraftrad was a veritable mini-tank, designed to carry three soldiers and their equipment as well as tow a trailer. It had two rear caterpillars and turned in the same way as a tank, by slowing or stopping one of the caterpillars; in this way, it could turn on the spot within a radius of 3m. The oversize, parallelogram, motorcycle-style front fork was limited to turns of less than 25° on a good surface.

As a historical aside, the HK 101 also had a heater intended to help with starting and to give the driver a little warmth. This blowlamp-like affair alone consumed around 10 litres of fuel per 100km!

The famous NSU Kettenkraftrad makes a reverse manoeuvre.

The year 1939: the final version of the Mercier was powered by a two-stroke, two-cylinder, 540cc Aubier-Dunne engine, which was apparently its only application on a motorbike. The cooling fan has gone, and the caterpillar mounting is back to flat-bar supports. Imagine trying to steer this using just the handlebars... (Daniel Tille Archive)

Designed to cope with the intense cold on the Russian Front, the Kettenkraftrad was not a great success.

In kit form for enthusiasts

So that's it for caterpillar bikes? No, certainly not, but military vehicles, designed to go anywhere, have often given rise to leisure or utility civilian developments. Thus from the caterpillar motorcycle would come the snowmobile. We are deliberately going to ignore the true snowmobiles with their double front skis, but there have been a few quite interesting machines based on motorbikes or scooters with rear caterpillars.

A curiosity of the 1982 Milan Show was this Montesa 349 trial bike, for which the Italian importer offered a ski to replace the front wheel. The rear gear was connected to a speed reducing gear, which drove the caterpillars via two side chains.

A test drive in the early 1920s.

T here's no doubt that our urban future lies with the non-polluting little electric scooter. Yet the idea is not new and there have been countless more or less successful attempts to create three- or four-wheeled electric-powered vehicles since the beginning of the 20th century. Two-wheeled examples have been much rarer.

The principle of the fuel cell, invented in Britain in 1802 by Sir Henry Davy, was put into practice 37 years later by another Englishman, Sir William Grove. In 1834, still in England, the first vehicle powered by an electric motor was built. The first electric three-wheeler, the Autoette Electric Car, appeared in the United States in 1852 and it seems that it was in France, in 1880–1881, that the first electric cars were produced, by Camille Faure and Jules Raffard, then by Charles Jeantaud.

But let's get back to our beloved motorbikes. The specialist Philippe Boursin tells of a tandem made in England in 1897 by Gladiator-Pingaud that covered a kilometre at 34kph, a record for the time, but was it actually a two-wheeled tandem? Two poor photos from the early 1920s depict the first tests of true electric bikes, but following these artisan beginnings, we have to wait until 1928 for the Lyon-built Électrocyclette, with its tubed frame, small wheels, chain transmission and a range of 30km. Five years later, in 1933, an electric-powered Favor appeared in the catalogue, but was not actually produced. Likewise with New Map, who in 1941 showed off their Paupe, a kind of electric scooter (also offered with a standard engine), the only known example of which is preserved in the Henri-Malartre Museum, near Lyon (at Rochetaillée-sur-Saône).

FIRST STEPS WITH ELECTRICITY (1928—1972) Our future's past

This bike was based on an ABC from the 1920s, whose wide double-cradle frame lent itself well to the task of carrying the huge batteries.

A family outing on a 1942 Socovel. The fuel tank has acquired its final shape, and the now solid wheels have fatter tyres. (Yves Campion Archive)

Socovel 1942

It was Belgium that witnessed the first mass-produced electric two-wheeler, in 1942 and 1943, the Socovel. Fuel had, of course, been rationed in Belgium under the German occupation since the spring of 1940, and this was what gave the Limelette brothers the idea of an electric motorcycle, in 1941. Three 6v batteries gave it a range of about 50km (30 miles) at a speed of 25–30km/h (15-20mph), and the Socovel was so successful that the factory cheated on its output quantity, reusing serial numbers so as to exceed the 500 authorised by the occupying authorities. On the other hand, deliberate dragging of feet prevented them from fulfilling the order from the German Army, who wanted to use the Socovel on its airfields!

Once the fuel shortage was over, the standard engine came back into its own and it wasn't until the early 1960s that a few electric scooters, intended for the disabled and often more like small cars, would reappear in Britain and the United States.

One of the first Socovel scooters built in 1941. The later versions would have bigger wheels and a boot whose fuel-tank-shaped top would lend it a more conventional appearance. (Amnéville Museum)

● ● ● ● Acec 0.5hp, later 1hp, electric motor supplied by 18v batteries (3 x 6v 45Ah) – Chain transmission – Double-cradle tubular frame without rear suspension – Parallelogram front suspension – 18in spoked wheels – Approx. weight 75kg – 25km/h (10mph) – Range approx. 50km – Recharge time 10 hours.

The American Sanders Messenger of 1966.

The electric Mobylette came so close to production that Motobécane made a series of publicity photos. Note the tapered tubes of the handlebars, inside which ran all the control cables!

The prototype without its fairings reveals its two big modified Citroën DS batteries and, behind, an extra-flat engine with forced-air cooling.

The target market was principally the young. Would this quiet, tame Mob' have won them over?

A bit of a jumble, but you can't help but admire the compactness, with the engine on one side (the other as we view it) and the bicycle chain on the right-hand side.

The front hub and its speedometer cable. Because of this, the brakes acted on the rim, like a bicycle.

● ● ● ● Flat, permanent-magnet motor and radial commutator, 1kW, 24v, 1.5kg – 2 x 12v lead batteries – Trussed tube and pressed frame – Brake blocks at the front, drum at the rear – Approx. 40kg – 60km range – 45km/h (28mph).

The electric scooter designed by Roger Paupe for New Map in 1942, provided with two Paris-Rhône 24v motors, would sadly not get as far as production. (Jean Bertin Collection)

An electric Mobylette in 1972

All the big automotive firms, whether making two-wheelers or four, are now working on electric power. The French 'Mobylette' showed the way... 38 years too soon!

The prototypes are so fascinating that they could have ended up forgotten, or had instant success the moment they appeared. Coming in the midst of the oil crisis, this interesting electric moped, designed in 1972 by Éric Jaulmes, the technical director at Motobécane, failed to get management backing. Probably a wise decision, as the market was not then ready to accept such a novelty, especially the younger segment that Motobécane was keen to capture.

The really clever thing about this prototype was the way it avoided the heavy power consumption normally required for starting. A sensor in the front wheel hub brought the motor into use only once the bike had been pedalled to a speed of 4–6kph. This device also avoided the motor stalling as a result of an excessive energy demand upon it. Another weight saving was with the batteries, which, in 1972, had to be the traditional, heavy lead-acid type: 'Why load up a light vehicle with 300Ah batteries with their internal grids and big terminals?' asked Éric Jaulmes. 'We gained 35% capacity by modifying two Citroën DS batteries (the first to replace the heavy Bakelite shell with a slimmer plastic one) and using a short, small-diameter cable.'

Very modern for its time, the flat engine specially designed by Novi, a subsidiary of Motobécane, sat behind the batteries. In the prototypes that were built, it transmitted power either through a short, direct chain, or via an automatic Shimano two-speed box (double belt transmission with double centrifugal clutch). The open frame with a wide, low-slung cradle also served to protect the batteries in the event of a crash.

But sadly, electricity did not yet have the weapons at its disposal to fight against the conventional two-wheeler. We have to await the arrival of the lighter and more powerful lithium batteries and soon, perhaps, the fuel cell...

An electric delivery tricycle in Paris, 1941.

A fine line-up of four Souplex 125 Luxe types in 1948. They boldly claimed a speed of 80kph! (Yves Campion Archive)

F

rom the dawn of motorcycling, the Belgians have turned out some superb machines. From the Escol to the Souplex, they have also come up with designs that are both comical and outlandish, though without being completely senseless. Under close consideration, the Souplexes even have something of a revolutionary character about them, being among the European pioneers of the mini-bike and of the light-alloy wheel.

SOUPLEX MOTORCYCLES (1939—1948)
The Belgian mini

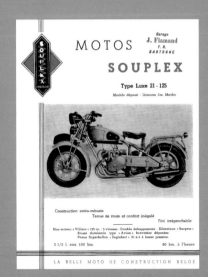

1948 catalogue.
(Yves Campion Archive)

The first October 1939 Souplex appears to have come straight off a fairground roundabout with its 12in wheels. In fact, the Souplexes were particularly popular with fairground people, especially on the wall of death, for which Menko offered a specially reinforced version. (Yves Campion Archive)

Impressed by the mini-bikes that had been built in the United States, Joseph Menko, a Brussels maker of industrial washing machines in the 1930s, constructed his first motorcycle in March 1939. It was fitted with small, 12in, aluminium, disc-hub wheels and powered by a 125cc, two-stroke Villiers engine angled towards the front so as to fit it in the curve of the frame. It was, to say the least, an odd arrangement in which only the shaped mudguards looked as if any aesthetic considerations had been applied to them, which unfortunately was not sufficient to make it stylish. The same year, Joseph Menko made a special version for a wealthy Belgian aviator, which was shorter, more compact and so much more attractive. It was just 80cm high and even possessed the luxury of a revolutionary rear swing suspension with two conical springs under the saddle, which were compressed by a rod articulated on the swingarm. The arrangement was similar to the one in use on most of today's

This 80cm model, specially built in late 1939 for the aviator Georges Hanet, has a triangular rear swingarm suspension bearing on a system of rods and compressing two conical springs. It was revolutionary in principle, but probably ineffective given the limited travel. (Yves Campion Archive)

sporting bikes, but the travel was so limited that the only point of this suspension would seem to have been to demonstrate the builder's skill.

Priceless luxury

Luxurious and expensive, these little Souplexes, fitted for the most part with 125cc, two-stroke Villiers engines, but occasionally with a Villiers 250cc, and a three-speed gearbox, were craftsman built without much consideration of cost. We are a long way here from the American philosophy where scooters and mini-bikes were, with a few exceptions, crude constructions made from a few tubes slung together, two wheels and a lawnmower-style, four-stroke, side-valve engine. Menko had rather nobler visions.

The second generation of Souplexes saw the introduction of superb alloy wheels very much inspired by Bugatti. Specially made for Joseph Menko, they were an almost unique feature at that time (with the exception of the Czech Böhmerland that had appeared in the mid-1920s) and would be retained until the final Souplex turned out in 1948, one of the characteristic features of the marque.

Other refinements were the front parallelogram suspension with Silentblock joints and the unusual telescopic rear suspension resting on leaf springs that were fitted to the flat twin models. Yes, there were twin-cylinder Souplexes, as well!

Was it because, back in 1924, Albert I, King of the Belgians and a former motorcyclist, owned a (Brussels-made) Jeecy-Vea with a Coventry Victor engine that, in 1946, Menko was attracted by the sumptuous 285 and 350cc, side-valve flat twins that the renascent British manufacturer had just brought out? It's a curious fact that these flat twins, with their separate gearbox and chain-driven secondary transmission, were not used by any other motorcycle manufacturer! On the Souplexes, they were attached to four-speed Albion gearboxes via an 'elastic joint', as the catalogue, with no further elaboration, tells us. Coventry Victor had promised that their early versions with separate gearbox would be followed by complete engine/gearbox units, but the absence of significant orders meant that the necessary investment was not forthcoming and the English manufacturer simply added a false crankcase to make it look like a single unit.

Joseph Menko also turned out a prototype with the whole bodywork in aluminium, but his ambitions were beginning to outgrow motorcycles. Since the war, this industrious Belgian genius had been harbouring the dream of building a car... a very special one, naturally. So, the construction of mini-bikes ceased in 1948, with 88 machines having been produced, although the Souplex had never got beyond the prototype stage. The adventure was over for good by 1951 and a frustrated Joseph Menko returned to washing machines. His preposterous two-stroke, four-cylinder horizontal engine intended for the car was never to appear.

Souplex is to our knowledge the only motorbike manufacturer to use the 1946 Coventry Victor flat-twin, side-valve engine in 285 and 340cc versions. The engine is matched to a separate Albion gearbox, and the secondary transmission is chain operated. Note the oil gauge fitted above the magneto and, above the gearbox, a large belt-driven dynamo. (Yves Campion Archive)

The 250cc version, still with a Villiers engine. (Yves Campion Archive)

The publicity leaflet shows the fitting of the removable-rim, alloy wheel.

Mini-shorts and mini-bikes in the elation of post-war days. (Yves Campion Archive)

Exclusively revealed here is the 1949, two-stroke, four-cylinder engine that was to be used in the Souplex car. The fan looks as if it comes from... a washing machine! No photos of the completed vehicle have come into our possession, and the project was abandoned in 1951... (Yves Campion Archive)

●●●● The brief renaissance of Coventry Victor

A pioneer of the flat twin since 1911, Coventry Victor appeared to give up on the motorcycle in 1935, turning instead to three-wheelers. English firms are nothing if not hardy and Coventry Victor reappeared at the 1946 London Show with a curious flat twin, offered in 285cc (55 x 60mm) and 340cc (60 x 60mm) versions, each one being (in theory!) available with liquid or air cooling. It is said the engine was designed in response to an Army bid to tender. It had a vertically split crankcase, with a one-piece crankshaft, an oil tank within the engine cases and side valves. To adapt the engine to the motorbike, in which it was arranged transversally, Jos Menko designed an angled drive via 'an elastic joint' and a chain transmission to the Burman gearbox.

Coventry Victor did not build the engine-gearbox unit they had promised. They cheated by enclosing both the little flat twin and its Albion four-speed box in one false aluminium casing. Sit back and admire the Duralumin Bugatti-style wheels and the rear telescopic suspension with leaf springs. On your marks, collectors, only ten were ever built! (Yves Campion Archive)

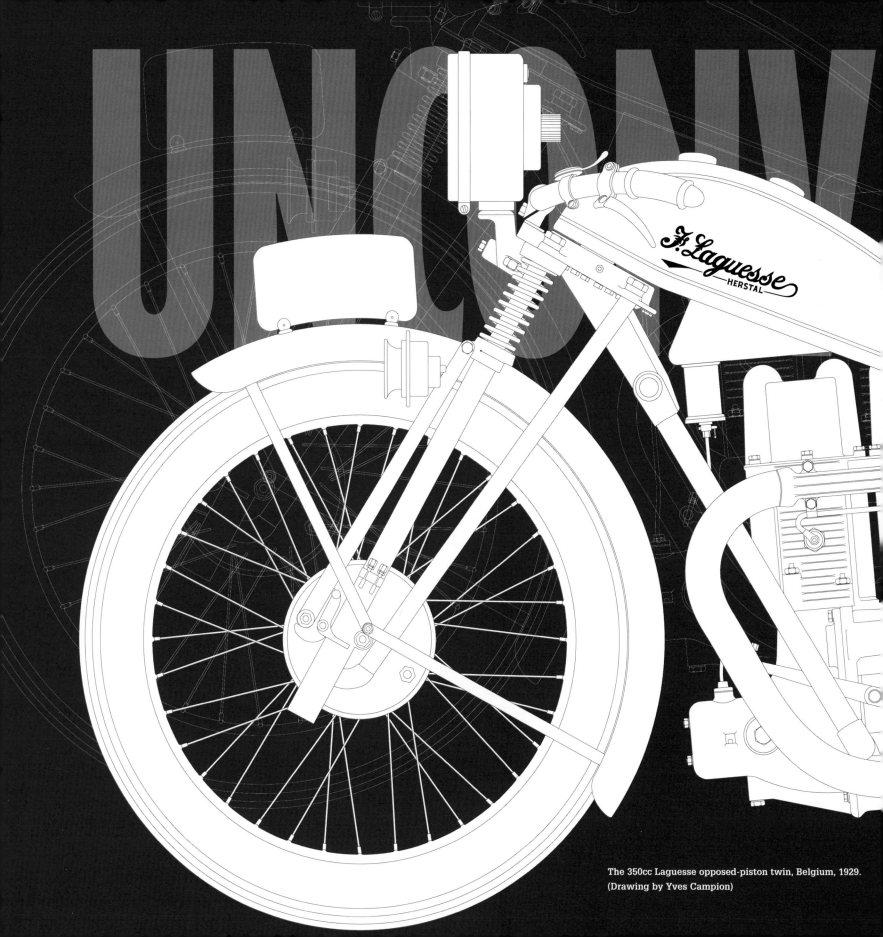

The 350cc Laguesse opposed-piston twin, Belgium, 1929.
(Drawing by Yves Campion)

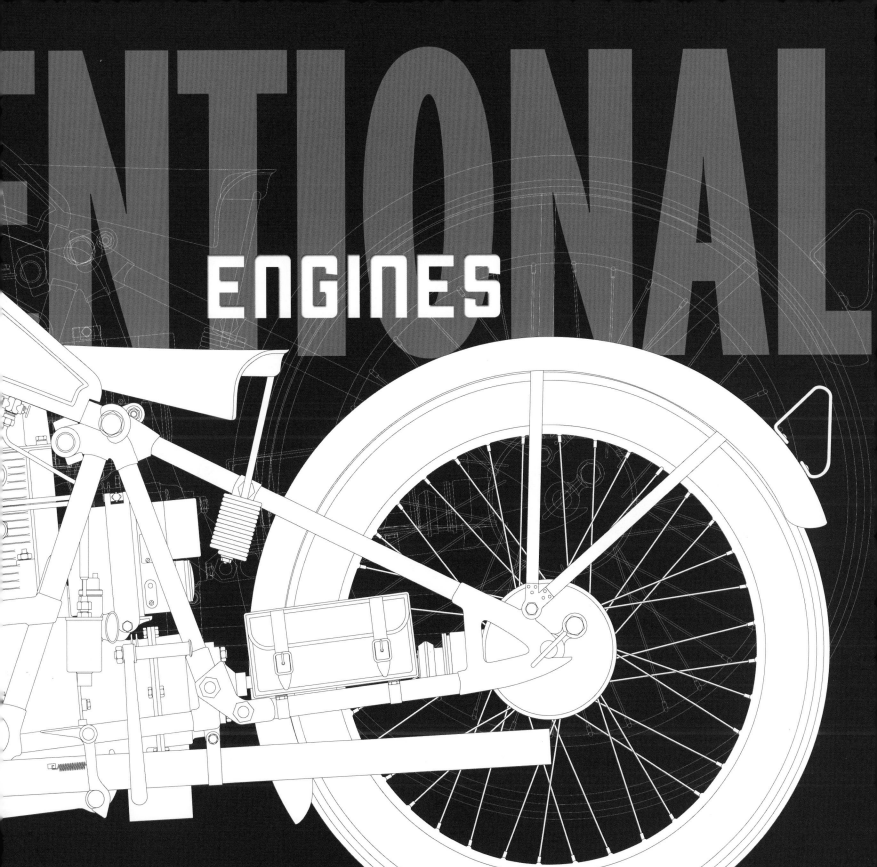

BALLOT ENGINE-BLOCK (1920)
The hand of Henry

Complete, but waiting to be restored, a 1921 Alcyon with a Ballot engine and the maker's typical front fork.

T he well-known engineer Ernest Henry, who in 1913 created the futurist, twin-cylinder, competition Peugeot 500 with DOHC and eight valves, would make only one more motorcycle after the war, a less prestigious project, but just as novel: the Ballot, displayed at the 1920 Paris Show.

This engine, from the Établissements Ballot (Paris, 14th) was to be their only incursion into two-wheelers. It was a family business, run by brothers Édouard and Maurice Ballot and well known since the early years of the century for its marine and submarine engines (hence the company's trademark of the letters EB, for Établissements Ballot, accompanied by an anchor). During the war, Ballot branched out into car engines and supplied engine parts to, among others, Delage, Licorne and Hispano. But Peugeot's numerous successes in competition irked the Ballot brothers, especially the highly acclaimed success of the Lion in the Indianapolis 500. Peugeot, who won the race in 1913, finished second and fourth in 1914, second again in 1915 then first in 1916, and announced that they would compete again in 1919. A new sort of phoney war broke out with Ballot having hired Ernest Henry, the designer of the twin-cam, eight-valve Peugeot, who in a few months came up with an eight-cylinder Ballot with the same features.

The 1919 Indianapolis race was yet again dominated by Peugeot, but the first Ballot car finished 11th and recorded the fastest lap. The following year, the Ballot would take first and fifth places. Perhaps as a diversion after his exuberant automobile creations, Ernest Henry designed an unusual motorcycle engine that was to be the first French two-stroke with the engine and gearbox in a single unit.

As usual, Henry goes for the unusual

Nothing about this engine was conventional. As with the Grand Prix Peugeot 500, there was a monobloc crankcase, this time separated into three compartments for the crankshaft, the magneto and the gearbox. Again like the Peugeot 500, there was a one-piece crankshaft with an assembled con-rod rotating on needles and, as on the Peugeot, the crankshaft could be taken out by removing a cover on the right-hand

side. Housed in the middle compartment, the magneto was driven, on the early models, by a sprocket engaged on the primary-transmission chain, which was an internal-toothed silent chain (much favoured by Honda, in particular, in later years). The tension was regulated by means of an eccentric gear. On the later models, including the Labor illustrated here, the silent chain was replaced by two simple chains, one for the primary transmission and the other for the dynamo. A further unusual feature was that the right-side aluminium footboard, pivoted at the front, served as the kick-start and, as it acted directly on the crankshaft, it allowed the novel feature of starting while in gear.

As if this batch of novelties was not enough, Ernest Henry had originally designed a gear change in which a padded forked lever would be manipulated left and right between the knees. No need to ask why this device would be replaced by a conventional gear lever on the production version! This unique engine was displayed in 1920 on an

Alcyon motorbike, then adopted in 1921 by all of Alcyon's subsidiary brands: Armor, La Française, Olympique, Jean Thomann and... Labor. An assembler rather than a builder, and a long-term part of the Alcyon group, this Courbevoie-based firm, situated in the suburbs of Paris from 1908 to 1959, mostly produced small-capacity, utility models, though there was the 500 Super-Sport of the 1930s.

Too modern, too complicated and much too expensive (2,600 francs when it first came out, or the cost of a good English 250 at the time), this unique Ballot-engined bike was produced in very limited numbers and would disappear from the catalogues in 1922. As for the Établissements Ballot, they were to be absorbed by Hispano-Suiza in 1931 and would finally close their doors in 1932.

Engine and gearbox are neatly combined in a single block. The connecting rods are accessed by opening the round hatch below the cylinder. The large rectangular hatch behind it allows removal of the magneto, whose circuit-breakers remain accessible even with the engine casing closed. The gearbox can be reached from the top.

The power unit is huge in relation to the cylinder capacity. The primary transmission, using a single chain on the production version, is enclosed in a sealed oil bath. The bulge at the front of the casing contains the kick-start mechanism.

●●●● Ballot two-stroke, single-cylinder engine-block, air cooled – 265.4cc (65 x 80mm) – Non-detachable head – Assembled connecting rod with roller bearings and crankshaft removable through the right side of the engine – Amac carburettor – Mixture lubrication and direct oil injection into the cylinder – Ignition from a magneto built into the block – Bronze-steel cone clutch – Footboard kick-start – Chain primary (enclosed) and secondary transmission – Two-speed, lever-operated gearbox – Single-cradle open frame – Parallelogram front fork – Drum front brakes, block on rim at the rear.

A conventional motorbike... but only from this angle!

The back of the footboard lifts and acts as a starter pedal.

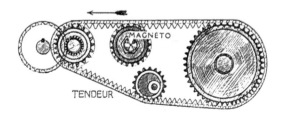

On the early models the primary transmission was entrusted to an internally toothed chain (Hy-Vo) that drove the magneto as well. The tension was maintained by an eccentric gear. (Jean Bourdache Archives)

Ernest Henry initially planned a gear changer with the knee moving a forked lever with knobs on the end from right to left. On the production run, this device was replaced by a conventional lever. (Jean Bourdache Archives)

The plate gives the impression that this was the 35,358th of these built. Don't believe it; production of the engine was limited.

STEPPED PISTONS (1919—1975) From Dunelt to Norton

The little Dunelt had some success in racing and created interest among other specialist two-stroke manufacturers. It is seen here festooned with laurels in 1927 with Lissmonde at the handlebars and behind, from left to right, Abram Neiman, the inventor of the anti-theft device, Albert Sourdot and Jean Gaussorgues, both Monet-Goyon champions.

Edwald Kluge, who would later exercise his talents as master of the supercharged two-stroke, DKW.

Weary, Dunelt threw in the towel in 1928 and abandoned stepped-piston two-strokes to devote themselves to 250 to 600cc four-strokes, until the end came in 1956.

Norton tries again

The idea was to re-emerge in 1971. Denis Poore, Norton's boss, wanted his engineers to work on a two-stroke bike to compete with the multi-cylinder Kawasakis and Suzukis. A small team led by Bernard Hooper (who had already distinguished himself in the creation of the Norton Commando) began work on the Wulf project, a joint enterprise between the British National Research Development Corporation and Norton Villiers. With typically British originality, this stepped-piston, 180° twin was no mere Dunelt remake, as it offered the additional advantage of doing away with the passage of the combustion mixture through the crankcase as was usual in two-stroke engines. On the Wulf, the mixture was admitted through the top of the large bore of the lower part of one piston and was compressed as the piston rose, pushing it into the combustion chamber at the top of the other cylinder. Proving too costly, the project was cancelled in 1975 as the Norton Villiers empire was collapsing, but Hooper continued to work on the concept in both diesel and petrol applications until the mid-1990s.

T he more gas you can let into the cylinder, the better. In pursuit of this principle, the history of engines is full of inventions designed to compress the gases before they are admitted to the combustion chamber. For two-strokes, one solution appeared ideal.

The principle consisted of making a stepped piston. The greater-diameter, lower part acted as a pump, compressing the gases, while the smaller-diameter, upper part served the conventional purpose of opening and closing the cylinder ports. However, nothing in this world is that simple.

The technique's specialist was Dunelt (from DUNford and ELlioT), set up in Birmingham in 1919, with a curious 450cc single-cylinder two-stroke that established the technology of pistons with two bores. Although in production until 1927, this ingenious and novel arrangement never really solved its inherent problems: heavy and tall, the stepped piston was tricky to build. It required large piston-to-bore tolerances because it distorted unevenly when hot and guiding it was difficult. Dunford and Elliot kept at it and in 1925 came up with a 250cc using the same principle, but partly avoiding some of its defects by use of a smaller piston. Furthermore, the 250 met with some racing success and was timed at 115km/h (71mph) in the capable hands of the noted

Much more effective than its big sister: the 1926 250cc Dunelt. (Sammy Miller Museum)

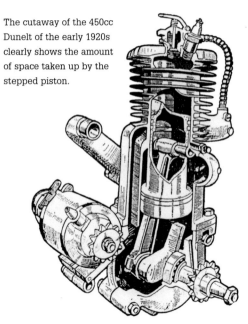

The cutaway of the 450cc Dunelt of the early 1920s clearly shows the amount of space taken up by the stepped piston.

Original to the last, Dunelt had the chaincase serve as the exhaust pipe on some models!

The Wulf makes a public appearance in 1975. A water-cooled version would follow.

Developed between 1971 and 1975, the Norton Wulf 500 had a two-cylinder engine set at 180° (bore: 74.5 and 105; stroke: 57mm) with two Amal carbs and valve admission in the largest section of the cylinders. The separate gearbox, driven by internal-tooth Hy-Vo chains, is bolted to the back of the engine. The pressed-steel frame was specially designed by Alec Issigonis, the creator of the famous Austin Mini.

FERNAND LAGUESSE'S OPPOSED PISTONS (1923—1931) Two pistons in one cylinder barrel

Jean Kicken on one of the first air-cooled versions, in 1923 or 1924. (Yves Campion Archive)

Second in the 1925 Belgian Grand Prix (pictured here), the Gillet-Laguesse henceforth has liquid cooling but still no supercharger. (Yves Campion Archive)

Normally, the gases admitted into the cylinder are compressed by a single piston. By putting one at each end of the cylinder, it should be twice as efficient. In theory!

Among the most brilliant applications of this theory established in the late 19th century by the German engineer Ochelhauser was the six-cylinder, two-stroke diesel with twelve opposed pistons on Junkers aircraft between 1915 and 1939. The 1932 Junkers Jumo 205 D, with its 16.6-litre cylinder capacity was the first engine to offer a weight-to-power ratio of less than 1 (0.67kg/hp).

In these engines, and those developed later by Fiat (in 1924 for a racing car), by Piaggio (in 1951 for the record-breaking Vespa) and by DKW (in 1947 for a 250cc racing bike), the cylinder, or cylinders had a crankshaft at each end. This was costly, took up space and was difficult to adjust, especially if, like Piaggio in 1951, you wanted to dispense with a supercharger and use the two crankcases for admission and pre-compression of the gases. In 1918, Garelli had simplified the concept by designing a twin-bore engine with a single crankshaft and this system was widely used by, among others, Puch.

Too simple for Fernand Laguesse

A renegade at the FN factory where he had worked between 1914 and 1918, the Belgian engineer Fernand Laguesse moved to Gillet where he designed the first 300 and 350cc models in 1920. He later persuaded Gillet d'Herstal to make a prototype with two Opposed Pistons in a single cylinder, logically named '2PO'. There was no second crankshaft here, but instead two external rods (one on each side of the central big-end bearing), in opposition to the master rod and transmitting the movement from the crankshaft below to the piston at the top. Apart from this addition, the engine was a conventional two-stroke. The cylinder, open at the

This view of the Gillet-Laguesse on one of its last appearances in 1927 clearly shows the supercharger and the exhaust lines. Note the state of the road that is being used as a circuit and, behind, a superb brand-new Monet-Goyon RCS 350. (Yves Campion Archive)

top, contained a very long, stepped piston whose lower part slid until it met the other piston. The large-diameter bore of the upper part held a spindle on which each of the connecting rods was mounted.

There were two exhaust ports, one at the front of the cylinder and one behind. Our friend Laguesse would build two versions of his PO, the first air-cooled and the second water-cooled. He even attempted to use a supercharger. The cycle parts are not to be dismissed either and, when all is said and done, very modern, with a fine triangular shape in straight tubes and a very long steering tube.

Powerful and efficient, the 350cc Gillet 2PO (54mm bore x 2 strokes of 75mm) achieved fine, though rare, successes including a Belgian speed record of 145km/h (90mph) over a kilometre in 1926 with the liquid-cooled version, while the second one achieved just 135km/h (84mph). The 2PO actually reached 156km/h (97mph) during one of the attempts, but this was not officially certified because of a faulty chronometer in one direction. Not helped by the poor quality of the materials available at the time, the 2PO broke down frequently and Léon Gillet decided to put an end to the costly experiment.

Undeterred, Fernand Laguesse set up his own business, Lamoco (Larguesse Motor and Co.) in Liège in 1927 and doubled the stakes this time by building an in-line, two-

cylinder bike, with each cylinder barrel taking two pistons, as on the Gillet. It had a capacity of 350cc (42mm bore x 2 x 62.5mm stroke for each cylinder) and the design was considerably modernised compared with the Gillet: connecting rods in Duralumin, induction by rotary valve, separate lubrication. There was a three-speed gearbox and the transmission was no longer by chain as on the Gillet, but by shaft. Equally up to date, the double-cradle frame had a revolutionary new telescopic fork. Through lack of funding, the project was curtailed after only three examples had been built. For all that, it didn't disappear as NSU bought the rights and continued the project, though it was ultimately fruitless.

September 1926: Jean Kicken, Gillet's test driver, on the liquid-cooled, supercharged Laguesse that had just taken the Belgian 350cc record at an average of 145km/h (90mph). Because of its height, the engine had to be placed at an angle. (Yves Campion Archive)

Setting off in 1927 for one of the Laguesse's last races in France, using transport typical of the time. (Yves Campion Archive)

The engineer Fernand Laguesse.
(Musée Communal d'Herstal Archive)

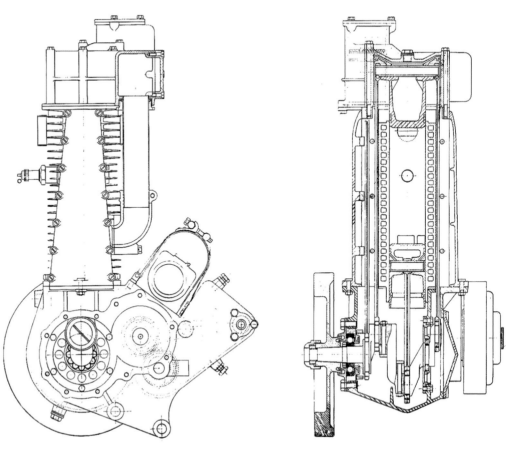

Cross sections of the 1925 single-cylinder Gillet-Laguesse in its air- and water-cooled versions. The upper piston uncovers the admission ports and lets in the gases that have been precompressed by a pump. The central spark plug ignites the mixture when the two pistons are at their top dead centre, and the lower piston uncovers the exhaust ports.

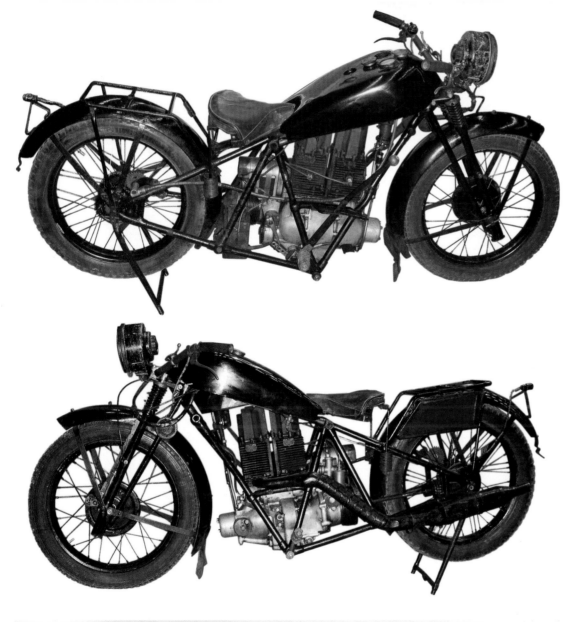

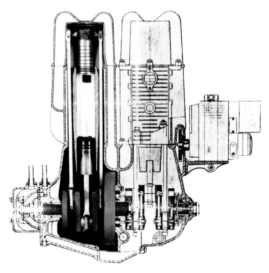

The 1929 Laguesse Lamoco with two cylinders (and four pistons), preserved in original condition.

Section of the 1929 two-cylinder Lamoco: this time there are two opposed-piston cylinders and admission is by rotary valve. This was a technique that had been mastered by Laguesse and used on the first 'Tour du Monde' Gillets.

The Lamoco was also noteworthy for its remarkable triangular frame and telescopic-fork front suspension.

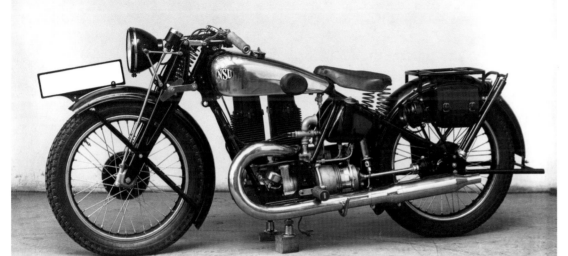

The 1931 NSU-Laguesse saw a return to conventional cycle parts. You can't innovate everywhere all the time! (Musée Communal d'Herstal Archive)

The 350cc prototype made by Laguesse for NSU in 1931. Intake is in the crankcase and a large-diameter pipe carries the exhaust from the two opposed-piston cylinders. (Musée Communal d'Herstal Archive)

RICHARD KÜCHEN'S ENGINES (1928—1955) The German King

The late 1935 range of Küchen engines for Ardie. From left to right, the 500 and 600cc side-valve power unit and engine on its own, an OHV 500, the superb 750 V-twin unit with shaft transmission that would sadly never see the light of day, the OHV 500/600cc sport and the two-stroke 200/250cc.

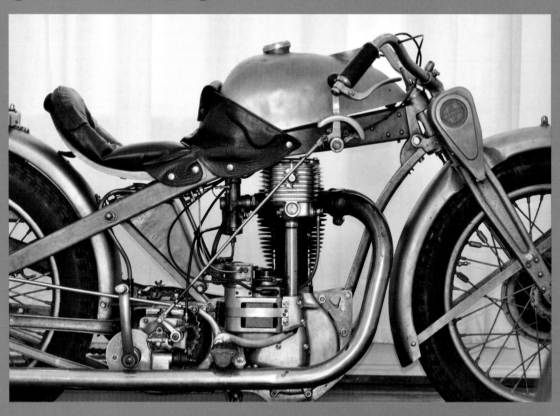

Elite-Werke, a maker of custom engines during the period 1925–1926, afterwards rendered its services to Opel in the building of the Motoclub with its Neander cycle parts and Kühne engine. It started manufacturing on its own account again in 1928, this time using face cam Kühne engines with three valves in 350, 500 and 600cc versions. Never put into mass production, the bike disappeared in 1930 after taking 24-hour national records and a victory in the German Bol d'Or.

Richard Küchen is one of the dozen or so men who have completely changed the world history of the motorcycle. Unconventional, original and eclectic, this brilliant engineer, born in 1898 at Bielefeld, was to design engines and motorcycles for more than a dozen German firms between the late 1920s and the mid-1950s.

An output of astonishing diversity, among which figure some of the most striking machines of their time. Richard Küchen, who set up his first factory at Saverne-la-Montagne, barely 10km from the French border, might easily have been French. Should this be a matter for regret? I am not sure that France would have given him so many opportunities to express himself!

In the early 1920s at a time when two-stroke was modern, Richard Küchen was thinking only about the development of four-stroke engines. Already very up to date with its SOHC driven by a vertical shaft, his first model K was distinguished by

Three types of valve gear tested by Richard Küchen in the late 1920s: three valves and a vertical cam (A), two valves with desmodromic control operated by a face cam (B) and a cylinder head with four valves (C) seen here in its desmodromic version.

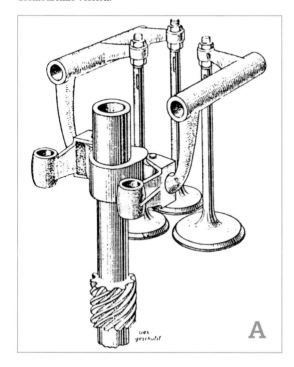

A

C

its fully enclosed valves, a rarity at the time, which would be one of the hallmarks of the early Küchen engines. From 1924, he used vertical cams on the shaft and rocker arms to operate the valves. Next, before Chater Lea, the high priest of this technology from 1927, he used simple or desmodromic faced cams operating two or four valves. Richard Küchen conscientiously tested and built almost every type of valve gearing possible on single-cylinder engines before opting (like Bugatti) for three valves (two for admission) with single or twin exhaust, either in an engine-block or an engine/gearbox unit. Wrestling with insurmountable problems of overheating and poor ignition, as the multiple valves prevented the use of a central spark plug, Küchen ended up, like everyone else, plumping for two valves per cylinder.

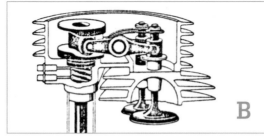

B

Along with his standard engines with separate gearbox, in 1929 Küchen also offered this fine engine-gearbox with a cylinder head having three parallel valves. Double ignition (the three valves prevented it from having a central spark plug) and a horizontally split crankcase. The photo was taken at the 1929 Paris Salon on the Picard stand.

The glory of the Nuremberg brands

In 1931, Küchen settled in Nuremberg with the aim of constructing a range of four-stroke engines for Triumph Werke (known as TWN outside Germany). That same year, Triumph also hired Otto Reitz from NSU, an act that upset Küchen, who departed for Zündapp, a company for whom he had already made engines in 1930. Here he was given the job of developing a completely new range of engines, aided by his younger brother Xaver, a technical and artistic designer. Zündapp was thus to become one of the principal German brands and at the 1933 Berlin Show they exhibited seven models, designed in record time by the Küchen brothers: all with pressed-metal frames, engines with very clean lines, chain-driven gearboxes and shaft transmission. The range consisted of two single-cylinder, two-stroke machines, the KK 200 and K 350, two four-stroke flat twins with side valves, the K 400 and K 500, two, four-stroke flat fours with side valves, the K 600 and K 800, and a 600cc, OHC, single-cylinder, shaft-driven model that was advertised in showrooms but never actually produced.

The Küchen style was thus born and all his creations were to be distinguished by a studied elegance, smooth lines and ample engine casings that wedded aesthetic style to ease of maintenance.

The K 400 and K 600 were soon dropped. On the other hand, the KK 200-equipped machine, which at that time in Germany did not require a driving licence and was tax exempt, met with considerable success, spawning further models, the economy BBK 200 with primary and secondary chain transmission, an even cheaper version, the DE 200 with a tubed frame, and finally the DB 200, which remained in production until the war.

The chain gearbox: an obsession

Gearboxes have always been the manufacturers' nightmare. The gears are very expensive to make and require tooling for which costs are not easily recouped. It is for this reason that separate gearboxes, built by specialist manufacturers were so successful. The other solution, adopted by the big firms, was to spread the costs by using the gearbox components in several different models. Richard Küchen, never one to follow custom, chose a third way: chain-operated gearboxes. Though undoubtedly slower than conventional geared boxes and a little heavier on maintenance, they had the advantage of being cheaper to manufacture and offered much greater flexibility between models. On all its 1933 range of models, Zündapp made a point of emphasising both the smoothness of its multiple duplex chain-driven transmissions and the fact that the transmission shaft was also able to absorb up to 10% of the torsion. Another notable feature of Zündapp engines was their one-piece forged crankshafts with assembled connecting rods mounted on caged needles (like Moto Guzzi).

One of the first of Richard Küchen's engines, a rocker-operated, three-valve 500cc, here used on a Herbi bike, built in Bohemia by the Herbig brothers in 1928 at Bad Liebwerda (now known as Lázně Libverda in the Czech Republic).

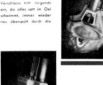

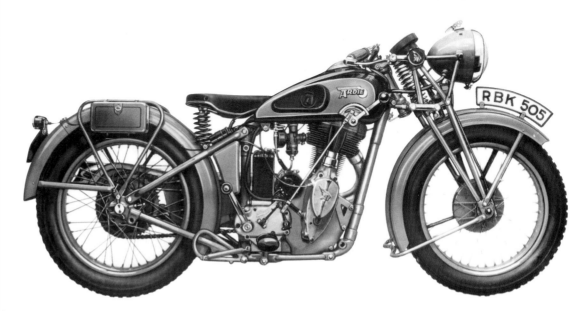

The magnificently styled Küchen Bauart engines of 1935 in 500 and 600cc versions. The pushrod OHV versions used on the Ardie RBK 505 are reminiscent of a shaft-driven SOHC, although it actually had a raised camshaft operating short push rods. Many motorbikes at the time still had valve gear open to the air!

The very modern 1939 Victoria KN 25 with a Horex-Columbus engine and four-speed gearbox developed a remarkable 18hp at 3,900rpm in the SN version and 20hp in this SS version with raised exhaust pipes. Some 4,000 civilian models were sold, as well as 6,000 Army KR models.

Of all the Küchen-engined Zündapps, which one should we show you? We've chosen the one that's generally least known, but with the biggest sales in Germany, the 1933 KK 200. Here it shows its chain gearbox with a shaft transmission without a universal joint as there was no rear suspension.

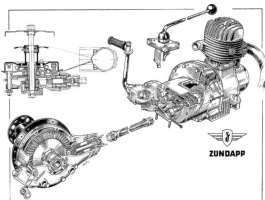

The discordant two-stroke

With the old two-stroke, single-cylinder Zündapps with their baffled pistons now becoming obsolete, the company asked Küchen to design a two-stroke engine to compete with the best, namely the flat-piston engines with Schnürle porting, for which the patents were held by DKW. Küchen unsuccessfully tried to get around these patents by inventing three-transfer porting (there were just two on the DKW design), in which the incoming gases passed through a divided transfer at the back of the cylinder, thus improving scavenging and hence performance. Production of the engine was started, but then stopped as it became clear that it still conflicted with the DKW patents. Richard Küchen then revisited an old idea first patented in 1899 by Joseph Magnat and Louis Debon, with a very unusual 250cc engine called the 'Gegenläufer'. This flat twin had four pistons opposed in pairs and driven by an unlikely system of connecting rods from a single crankshaft located underneath. It was never put into production and it appears that the somewhat irascible Küchen decided to leave Zündapp for DKW, spending two years there from 1934 to 1936. There, he developed his ideas on scavenging in two-stroke engines and was, presumably, involved in the early stages of the DKW Gegenläufer designed along the same lines, with four pistons opposed in pairs in two cylinders, though this time with a separate crankshaft on each side of the flat four.

A visionary engineer

It's hard to keep up with Richard Küchen over his meteoric and eventful career. In late 1936 he returned to Nuremberg, this time to Victoria, which was in a bad way. The firm had just stopped making the flat twins it had been building for 12 years, and importing the Sturmey Archer engines used in several models: its new 500 KR 8 and KR 9 two-cylinder Fahrmeister

had been a complete disaster. In collaboration with Hermann Reeb, the chief engineer at Horex, Richard Küchen developed the 350cc OHV Columbus, which was to be produced by Horex-Columbus-Werke and used by Victoria in its KR 35 SN and 35 SS models, followed by the 35 KR during the war. From 1938, the engine was also used in the Horex SB 35, which after the war would give birth to the Horex Regina, a best seller in Germany during the 1950s. Küchen also designed some smaller two-stroke engines at Victoria and turned out a complete range for Ardie in the 1930s, with some very fine high-camshaft OHV design on 500 and 600 singles and a 750cc transverse V-twin being particularly worthy of mention. The build-up to war unfortunately put an end to these latter plans and Küchen returned to Zündapp in 1938 to design the KS 750 with a powered sidecar, based on the KS 600, the 'baby' he had left on his previous spell with them. For the Army, he designed the Goliath, a sort of remote-controlled mini-tank, powered by an electric motor, followed by the flat twin for the Zündapp K 500, while working at the same time on a two-stroke 125cc double-piston engine for the post-war period.

Once hostilities were over, he and his brother set up a design office at Ingolstadt, revisiting his idea for a transverse V engine, which he sold to Victoria. From this came the very fine Bergmeister, although it was never much of a commercial success.

Eclectic by nature, Küchen also turned out two-stroke 50ccs (Express), as well as four-stroke flat twins (Hoffmann Gouverneur 350), a two-stroke 250cc with a double piston for FN (the 175cc M 22), car engines and, to cap it all, a neat little four-stroke, 250cc, 360° vertical twin with very modern distribution via a chain-driven SOHC, which would (briefly) be used on the 1954 Tomax SV and the 1955 Motosacoche Opti. This appears to have been Richard Küchen's last significant work and he died at Ingolstadt on 5 October 1975.

In 1935, this fine V-twin unit with shaft drive transmission was truly revolutionary. Available in 600 and 750cc capacities, it used the same all-chain gearbox as was developed for Zündapp.

1954: Küchen adopted a new genre, the flat twin, with this fine OHV engine made for the Hoffmann Gouverneur in 250 and then 300cc versions.

The ultimate styling exercise in 1954–1955: a 14hp 250cc parallel twin with single chain-driven OHC. It was used by Tornax, UT and Motosacoche.

Brought out in 1952, the attractive Victoria Bergmeister would serve as the basis for the Japanese Lilacs. Pictured is the 1955 ISDT works version, which still has the red marks intended to stop changing of parts during a race.

Richard Küchen even had a try at two-stroke, double-piston engines with this 250cc model designed in 1953 for the FN M22.

Four cylinders, shaft transmission, super-comfortable suspension and a 250cc, narrow, flat twin with side valves... the FN 500 M18 might have been the best Grand Tourer of its time. Look at the style of the exhaust and inlet manifolds forming a finned ring around the cylinders.

A transverse boxer engine is a logical arrangement, being balanced, compact and well ventilated... but would two engines, one above the other, be better than one?

The classic flat-four design is where the two cylinders on each side are laid out one behind the other, leading to problems with the rear cylinders overheating. Other than liquid cooling, a solution is not easy to come by. Among the rare makes of motorcycle that have had a go at the flat four, only two notable examples have retained air cooling: the Zündapp K 800 in the late 1930s and the BFG from the early 1980s (using, it has to be said, a very effective forced-air system for its Citroën engine).

There is, however, another possible arrangement: two flat twins set out in an H form, one above the other!

On reflection, the idea seems less appealing as it requires two crankshafts and a seriously elevated centre of gravity. Nevertheless, three manufacturers had a try at this, although without any real success.

Brough Superior: a golden dream

The first into the ring was Brough Superior. The manufacturer, who tried a whole range of different engine arrangements, and was well known for its V-twins, exhibited the extraordinary Dream 1,000cc at the 1938

DOUBLE FLAT TWINS (1938—1954)
Are two better than one?

This second version of the FN trailing-arm fork looks almost conventional with its two tubes, resembling a telescopic fork, which carry on each side the triangles (upper tubes curved and lower straight) on which the swingarm pivots. Rubber Neiman rings absorb the shocks and the two false dampers behind the false fork are simply guides. It's the same at the back: telescopic guides for the arm and rubber rings for damping.

A sensation at the 1938 London Show, this Brough Superior Golden Dream (one of two incomplete survivors) continues in a starring role at the National Motorcycle Museum in Birmingham.

Stylish, luxurious and solidly built, the Brough Superior Golden Dream might have become the ideal GT, but it arrived just before the war!

London show, a bike that soon gained the name of 'Golden Dream' by virtue of its gold paintwork. It was a luxury liner of a bike, with two crankshafts, one above the other. Only a few were ever produced, and the Golden Dream was to remain at the showroom-prototype stage, a role it continues to play as one of the stars at the National Motorcycle Museum in Birmingham.

The 996cc (71 x 63), four-cylinder 'H' engine was air-cooled OHV, fed by twin carbs. The foot-operated gearbox had three speeds and the transmission was by shaft and worm-gear, despite this being less efficient than bevel gears. The cycle parts were typical of the manufacturer, with a double-cradle frame, Castle-type leading-link front suspension and telescopic at the rear. The weight was never divulged... perhaps it's just as well!

FN returns to four cylinders after an absence of 22 years

It was not until just after the war, in 1948, that the idea of the flat-four 'H' arrangement made its appearance again, in Britain and Belgium.

FN, the pioneer of four-cylinder motorbikes from 1904 to 1926, returned to the concept with a 500cc bike powered by an engine with two flat twins, one above the other, whose conventionally geared crankshafts turned in opposite directions (as on the Brough), thus eliminating the usual reverse-coupling required on engines that had the crankshaft laid out along the bike's axis. The engine-block was solid, in the classic FN style, but very narrow thanks to the side valves and the low, 125cc capacity of each cylinder.

The rather fanciful M18 even had pretensions to style

with its finned, aluminium exhaust and induction manifolds enclosing the left and right pairs of cylinders, linking the exhaust, at the front, and the induction, at the rear, to the carburettors and silencer. The secondary transmission was, logically enough, entrusted to a shaft. This was a technology that FN had fully mastered with its huge 1,000cc M13 flat twins, during the war.

The modern cycle part consisted of a wide double-cradle tubed frame, which made use of the tried and tested trailing-link and rubber-ring front suspension from the 250cc and 450cc M13 series from 1947. Here, in its second version, it was a little more conventional, with a fixed support tube imitating a telescopic fork. As on the 1949 OHC 500 motocross bike, the M18 was fitted with two guides on the long swing arm (behind the two support tubes) which, despite appearances and what has often been written, had no shock-absorbing function.

The rear was equally advanced, with swing-arm suspension dampened by rubber rings and provided, as at the front, with telescopic guides. It was solid and heavy, but the M18 would surely have been up for the title of most comfortable Grand Touring bike... if it had ever been produced!

The Wooler 500 Four of 1948: just 105kg for four cylinders!

John Wooler, one of the craziest British manufacturers, started out strongly in 1909 with a two-stroke 350 with a horizontal cylinder and double-action piston. The piston was driven by two external connecting rods and its lower face pre-compressed the gases in the cylinder housing. The first of John Wooler's bikes to be produced saw the light of day in his London workshops in 1911, a two-stroke, 230cc model with telescopic front and rear suspension and a frame with a patented device for dampening vibration. Increased to 344cc, it was produced by Wilkinson under the Wilkinson-Wooler brand. From 1919, Wooler made his name with some quite advanced 350cc and 500cc longwise flat twins complete with full suspension. Their black and bright yellow paint scheme and fuel tanks that extended forward to enclose the steering column quickly earned them the soubriquet of 'flying bananas'. The success of these reliable and comfortable machines was, unfortunately, short-lived and John Wooler temporarily closed down in 1930.

However, he did not lose heart and during the war worked on plans for an unusual 500cc, flat four with two pairs of cylinders, one over the other. The engine was shown off in 1945 and a prototype was finally exhibited at the 1948 London Show. Wooler had surpassed himself: his four-cylinder bike was designed around a single-cylinder connecting-rod assembly, whose connecting rod drove an unlikely collection of four other rods, two of which were forked. Wooler thus created the lightest 500cc four-cylinder ever built: just 105kg, only 28.5kg of which was the engine!

The two pairs of cylinders on top of each other give the 1948 prototype Wooler an excessively high centre of gravity.

Clever and very finely made, the Wooler connecting-rod assembly of 1945–1948 is based on a single-cylinder crankshaft working with a system of rods. (Sammy Miller Museum)

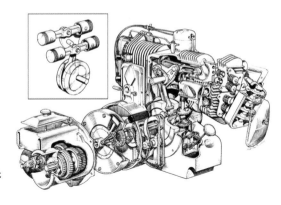

Seen from the rear it is clear why the 1948 Wooler engine is so light. The light-alloy cylinder block/head is mounted on a single-cylinder lower engine. (Drawing from *Motor Cycle*)

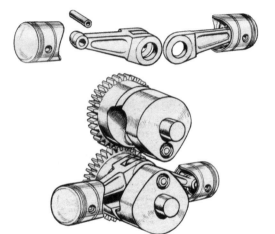

Brough Superior Golden Dream: The H-engine technology is expensive, but the balance is perfect thanks to the two crankshafts turning in opposite directions, with the 'knife and fork' big-ends allowing the left and right cylinders to be in alignment.

Eventually going on show in London at the end of 1954 after years of announcements and delays, the 1954 Wooler cost £294, practically the same price as an Ariel 1000 Square Four, but over £80 more expensive than a Triumph 500 Speed Twin at £210.

Modern and functional, only six of this final 1953–1954 four-cylinder 500 were made.

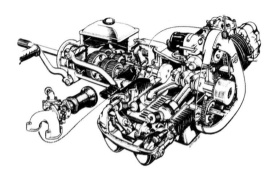

The 1954 Wooler flat four is quite conventional, were it not for the forked connecting rods on the front left and rear right pistons allowing the right and left cylinders to be perfectly aligned. (Drawing from *Motor Cycle*)

The 1954 Wooler 500 Four: the last 'banana'

Handicapped by its high centre of gravity, the ill-defined 1948 500 didn't get beyond the test stage. Having got his fingers burnt, John Wooler started work again in 1953 on the WFF 1, a flat four with classically stylish lines and excellent balance, which showed considerable promise. The two pairs of cylinders with OHV heads were now arranged one behind the other and the four-speed gearbox had shaft and bevel-gear transmission. Despite its complexity, this latest Wooler Four was still very light: 158kg as against the BMW R50's 195kg. To achieve perfect balance, Wooler had (like Brough Superior) used forked connecting rods on two of the cylinders, so that the pistons were perfectly opposed to each other and not offset as on the BMWs. The crankshaft turned on three bearings, with one in the middle, all mounted, like the connecting rods, on bushes. Wooler's signature feature of the extended fuel tank incorporating the headlight was retained, necessitating the design of a telescopic fork whose shoulder lacked the upper yoke. At the back, the telescopic suspension of the early versions was replaced on the final prototypes by a standard swingarm with two dampers. A small but pleasing mechanical detail was that Wooler reintroduced on this model the same idea as on both his first four-cylinder bike in 1945 and the 1954 model of using just three different sizes of bolt throughout, so as to simplify maintenance as much as possible. A screwdriver and two spanners were all that was needed for any operation, said Wooler, who nevertheless saw fit to provide a full tool-kit above the gearbox casing.

Ron Wooler, John's son, covered thousands of miles in tests. The machine performed superbly, developing 32hp at 6,000rpm and achieving a maximum speed of 160kph, but Wooler failed to raise the money needed to put it into production and the project ended with his death, in 1954.

The WM 350, seen here at the Lyon Fair in 1947, had a claimed output of 17hp at 6,000rpm and a speed of 125kph! (Gnome & Rhône Association Archive)

G nome & Rhône, the pre-war king of large-capacity French motorcycles, attempted to regain its lead after the conflict by reinventing the mechanical concept of the motorcycle. The dream was to turn into a nightmare.

Nationalised in 1945, Gnome & Rhône became Snecma and while its first priority was aircraft engines, particularly the jet engines on which it would build its success, motorcycle production continued. The 100cc R1 that saw the light of day in 1941 became the 125 R2 at the 1946 Paris Show where a surprise awaited visitors: a rather curious two-stroke 350cc with two double pistons arranged in a square. It was the first big post-war novelty and was announced by Gaston Durand, the technical director of the motorbike division, as in production and ready to appear in international competitions.

Four cylinders and just two sets of bearings for the engine and gearbox

Of a somewhat odd appearance, the very compact engine-block of the WM was as wide as it was long with two oval-shaped, widely spaced cylinder blocks, inclined towards the front and fed by a unique central carburettor.

It was a strange beast, the reason for which was said to be economy of construction. In about June 1944, Gaston Durand and the Russian Prince Igor Trubetzkoy (also a fine engineer and Simca-Gordini racing driver in 1947, later driving the first Ferraris) started with a blank sheet with the aim of building an engine intended to give the ideal balance between production costs and power output. Quite a tall order: to make something simpler using fewer parts meant giving each part more functions! However, the Franco-Russian pair won their challenge, producing a four-cylinder arrangement consisting of only two shafts and two sets of bearings for both the engine *and* the gearbox!

THE UTOPIA OF THE DOUBLE PISTON [1946] The Gnome & Rhône WM 350

This cutaway engine, on display at Snecma's Safran Museum in Melun-Villaroche, shows its very widely separated double pistons.

The large cap with the Snecma-GR logo gives access to the magneto. In front of it is the forward-acting kick-start.

On show in 1946: a mini four-cylinder bike with a sealed chain casing and a German-style front-suspended saddle. (Gnome & Rhône Association Archive)

So what was the trick? Each end of the front shaft carried an offset rod assembly (set at 180°), with two connecting rods mounted on the same crankpin. Each of the two-finned engine-blocks thus contained two cylinders with a common combustion chamber following the established principle of uniflow scavenging.

Between the two cylinders, the splined shaft served the purpose of being the main shaft for the gearbox and carried three gears engaging with a matching idling set on the hollow secondary shaft. A sliding notched spindle inside engaged with studs thus locking the selected gear ratio. Whether just fanciful or completely unhinged, the two engineers even came up with an electromagnetic gear-change system (with no clutch either) operated by a revolving handle. A large magneto driven by gears at the rear of the two engine shafts powered the system. They also considered a shaft transmission, but such fine ideas were quickly forgotten and the 350 WM that appeared at the 1946 Show had a conventional foot gear change and a chain final drive with a splendid, expensive, aluminium sealed casing.

Prince Igor's supercharger

But matters didn't rest there. There was a new patent, in late 1948, for a larger-diameter piston attached to a connecting rod pivoting on the main rod. Interviewed not long before his death in 2008, Prince Igor had even admitted considering a proper lobed supercharger placed above the gearbox.

In short, the WM promised a big reduction in the number of parts, a substantial simplification and a corresponding reduction in production costs. But the reality was rather different. As is usual when the way is being cleared for new technologies, research and testing were both protracted and costly (over 17 million francs). They were also a complete disaster. The offset rods were unable to bear the stresses and nor was the frame, though this was of conventional design. Gnome & Rhône, undergoing restructuring at the time, placed the blame on Gaston Durand, who, made redundant in 1950 for having wasted taxpayers' money, was taken on by Agache, the boss at Ydral, with a successful outcome. The 350 WM ended its days at the Garac engineering school in Argenteuil, presumably as a lesson in how not to do things.

Curious, but very compact from this angle. Each double cylinder has two cantilevered connecting rods.

La SNECMA présente sa nouvelle motocyclette "Gnome Rhône"...

SOCIÉTÉ NATIONALE D'ÉTUDE ET DE CONSTRUCTION DE MOTEURS D'AVIATION

150, Boulevard Haussmann - Paris-(8e) Carnot 33-94
Magasin : 49, Avenue de la Grande-Armée Kléber 90-56

The extravagant 1946 catalogue.

● ● ● ● Two-stroke, double-piston engine – 344cc – Bore x stroke: 42 x 62mm – Fuel feed via single Zénith carburettor – 17hp at 6,000rpm – Magneto ignition – Three-speed gearbox operated by handlebar twist grip – Multidisc clutch in oil bath – Sealed-chain transmission – Tubed, double-cradle frame – Telescopic front suspension – 19in wheels – 125kph.

...modèle 350cm³ type WM
2 temps - 2 cylindres - 4 pistons

3 VITESSES – SÉLECTEUR AU PIED
FOURCHE TÉLESCOPIQUE
CARTER DE CHAINE ÉTANCHE
VITESSE **120 KM HEURE** ENVIRON
CONSOMMATION : **3 LITRES 1/2** ENVIRON
A LA MOYENNE DE **70 KM HEURE**

La SNECMA construit également le Vélomoteur "Gnome Rhône" 125cm³ 2 temps type R2

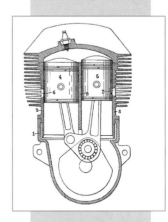

The last patent from 1948 with the rear piston of greater diameter.

The 1952 version of the Ultima photographed in front of Fargeton's house. An aluminium extension forward from the fuel tank covers the whole of the front, with two slots to allow the handlebars through. There is no longer any rear suspension. Note the transparent inspection hole on the OHC covers.

ULTIMA HORIZONTAL TWIN (1951)

The 'Arsenal'

For Fernand Fargeton, the manager of the design department at the Lyon motorcycle manufacturer, Ultima, nothing was impossible. When his racing driver friend Aimé Despland wanted the best sidecar available, the easiest answer was to build it himself. Thus was born this fantastic and unique Ultima, one of the first four-stroke horizontal twins ever made.

In the immediate post-war period, Fernand Fargeton, the son of one of Ultima's pioneers, produced single-cylinder 350 and 500 bikes with SOHC, as well as one four-cylinder bike consisting of four two-stroke monos linked in a square format.

In 1948, he and Aimé Despland, a Lyon sidecar racer who was financing the project, decided to build from scratch a 600cc sidecar unit. The Ultima director Eugène Billion, whose firm was in financial difficulties, though not officially backing the project, allowed his workshops to be used outside working hours. Having considered putting together two Velocette KTT units, the two colleagues eventually decided to build the engine themselves. They named it the 'Arsenal', a 600cc, four-stroke, parallel and horizontal twin-cylinder engine with DOHC driven by two shafts and bevel gears as in the 1938 supercharged NSU 350/500. The engineering was magnificent, but the concept was so far ahead of its time that it would not be commercially successful for another 50 years.

The 1951 version at the Coupes du Salon at Montlhéry. Standing behind, Fernand Fargeton (in the dark glasses) and Aimé Despland to his right, show how low-slung the machine is. Note the oil-pneumatic shock absorbers with their air inflation valves.

The 1952 version with its Imperial sidecar.
(Claude Bataille)

It was, in fact, one of the first four-stroke, two-cylinder horizontal designs in history. With the exception of the prestigious Hildebrand & Wolfmüller of 1894, with its unusual arrangement of the rear wheel acting as the crankshaft, this layout didn't reappear until the AJS Porcupine 500 of 1947. The Ultima 500 made its debut on the racetracks in 1951 and the horizontal twin concept was taken up again in 1969 with the Linto 500 based on a pair of Aermacchi 250cc OHV engines. It was then not until 2000 with the Yamaha T-Max 500 that this four-stroke engine arrangement was seen for the first time in mass production.

The reason for this lack of interest was simple: its size. The addition of a gearbox and the four-stroke's voluminous cylinder head made the wheelbase unreasonably long. This problem, resolved on the T-Max by the compactness of a modern engine and a scooter's small wheels, didn't matter on the Ultima, which was intended only for sidecar racing where a long wheelbase is rather an advantage and low height a necessity.

No luck

Unfortunately, the superb 600cc designed by Fargeton and Despland was barely ready when a new sidecar ruling banned superchargers and limited engine capacity to 500cc. It was therefore in this new form that the unit made its appearance at the Coupes du Salon, Montlhéry, in October 1951. The engine, though looking enormous, actually weighed only 55kg with its twin carbs and magneto, although this was admittedly without the gearbox and primary transmission. Its 70 x 64.5mm dimensions allowed it to develop its maximum output of 48hp, a running speed of 8,200rpm, a very high figure for the time. Unfortunately, lubricating oils at the time were still not of the best, and despite an oversized oil pump visible below the two OHC drive shafts, the Ultima had to abandon its first race because of lubrication problems.

Thanks to the horizontal engine, the rather contorted double-cradle frame was very low, with its constituent elements bolted together for easy dismantling, but it did not distinguish itself by its rigidity in the first version that was fitted with a rear swingarm suspension with two dampers. Desperate times call for desperate measures: the 1952 version, still with a bolted double-cradle frame abandoned the rear suspension and the opportunity was taken to increase the oil-tank capacity. Sadly, it was not enough. Though starting with a good idea, there weren't the funds to develop the 'Arsenal', and the big manufacturers came back in force before it had had the time to make its mark. It went to the regional racer, Roger Besse, and soon disappeared from the race tracks. Who knows, perhaps it will be back one day, in France's Coupes Moto Légende festival, for example!

●●●● Four-stroke, two-cylinder horizontal engine – Two SOHCs driven by shafts and bevel gears – 48hp at 8,200rpm – Dry-sump lubrication – Separate four-speed gearbox – Chain primary and secondary transmission – Bolted double-cradle tube frame – Oil-pneumatic suspension: telescopic at front, rear swingarm with twin shocks in 1951, rigid frame in 1952 – Single-cam double brakes at the front – 165kg – Speed with sidecar: 150km/h (93mph).

The 1952 version again. Still very tortuous around the front, the frame consists of bolted sections with the right tube passing between the cylinder and the OHC upper-bevel drive case. Note the size of the oil pump behind the OHC-drive, the different gearbox and the larger oil tank.
(Claude Bataille)

RACING
MOTORCYCLES

4

A twin-cylinder 500cc Peugeot Grand Prix with DOHC,
France 1922. (Drawing by Yves Campion)

PEUGEOT GRAND PRIX 500
Twin-cylinder bikes to change the world

DOHC [1913-1923]
A revolution with DOHC and eight valves

The fabulous Peugeot twin-cylinder motorcycles with double or single overhead camshafts truly invented the modern vertical twin and still make us dream today. Let us pay tribute.

The story begins in 1911, with the arrival of a 26-year-old Swiss engineer at Peugeot. By a strange quirk of history, the first Peugeot in 1901 was powered by a Swiss ZL engine, and it was again to be a Swiss who would re-establish their pedigree. Ernest Henry, who began his career in Geneva at the Picker-Moccand engine plant, arrived at an opportune moment. Peugeot was heavily involved in car racing and the engine he designed would hand them complete domination between 1912 and 1914, even including a stunning victory at Indianapolis in 1913. With an output of 148hp at 2,200rpm (albeit with an engine capacity of 7.6 litres!) in its 1912 version, the four-cylinder engine was a real revolution: it was the first to have both four valves per cylinder and double overhead camshafts. The cylinders and hemispherical cylinder heads were made in one piece, the overhead camshafts were driven by a gear train, and there was dry-sump lubrication.

Henry used this concept, the most advanced of its time, in every engine capacity and all applications, sometimes even with desmodromic distribution. Out of the twin-shaft, four-valve per cylinder series grew a 500 twin in 1913 for racing bikes, then an aeronautical V8 in 1915, of which more than 1,000 would be produced.

Sadly, though the cars driven by the formidable Boillot–Goux–Zuccarelli team would cover themselves in glory from 1912, the avant-garde 500 M motorcycle was to have a rather more chaotic debut to its career, and its air cooling, a source of much distortion, would make it much less robust than the liquid-cooled, four-cylinder cars.

From cars to motorbikes

The construction engine had the two cylinders with integral heads. As much as the engine was revolutionary, the transmission was a retrograde step, even with its reduction gearing that allowed the use of a small-diameter pulley wheel, thus reducing slippage. The cycle parts were hardly very modern either. But it didn't matter. Peugeot created a sensation on 5 April 1914 when it lined up three DOHC 500s on the Rambouillet track. Alas, the waterlogged track didn't suit these heavy 500s without gearboxes, which also probably needed further development. The favourite, Paul Péan,

1913: the Henry version which, in Péan's hands, covered the flying kilometre at an average of 122km/h (75.8mph) on 14 June 1914 at Achères.

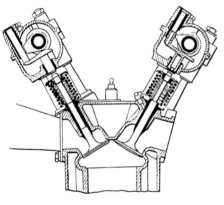

The tappet system used on the pre-war eight-valve versions and the cars designed by Henry.

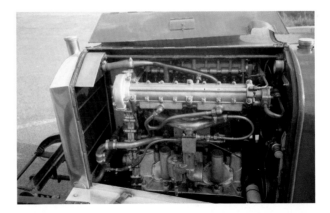

The DOHC with eight valves per cylinder in its liquid-cooled car version.

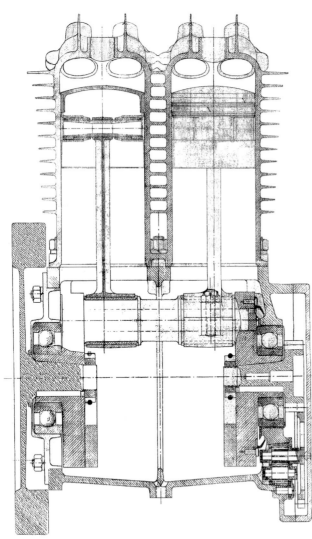

Eight valves, DOHC. The design of the 1913 Peugeot motorbike was revolutionary, as was its manufacture with the search for lightness pushed to the extreme: one-piece crankcase, steel rather than cast-iron pistons for superior accuracy and the smallest-possible-diameter bolts.

The second 1913 variant. The engine was rather handicapped by its old-fashioned transmission with gears and belt on to the back wheel. A 15-tooth gear at engine output (1) drives a 30-tooth idling gear (2) that in turn engages with another one of 30 teeth on an intermediate shaft (3). This shaft carries a cottered gear that drives the valve gear train and, at its left end, the front pulley of the secondary belt transmission. The gear on the intermediate shaft (3) also engages with another gear (4) of the same size for the magneto. A gear (5) for the oil pump is driven off the engine exit gear (1). Opposite this gear is the unmachined location for the first-version oil pump. (Jean Boulicot Collection)

The fabulous replica made by Jean Boulicot: ten years of work!

This sophisticated engineering is amazingly simple in construction: integral heads (a rarity for an overhead-valve engine, shared with the Bugattis, the Panhard flat twins and the Guzzi V8) and unit construction of engine and gearbox. Imagine the ordeal of changing a valve! Disconnect the connecting rods via the two access hatches provided under the engine casing. Take out the valve gear, remove the cylinder block with its rods and pistons. With the head being hemispherical, you have to remove the guide so that it can be tilted to a certain angle to get it out. Finally, take out the cottered wheel, the cover from the side of the engine casing and then the crankshaft!

abandoned the race with a frame cracked in two places, and Desvaux, the only one to finish on a 500, had a pyrrhic victory, covering the 400km at an average speed of 53.9km/h (33.5mph); meanwhile, on a no less revolutionary single-cylinder Alcyon 350, with four radial valves, Peugeot's sworn enemy won its category at an average of 58.8km/h (36.5mph)! Still, the 'Day of Records' held at Achères in June 1914 gave Peugeot the opportunity to regain its laurels, before the outbreak of war, with the terrific flying kilometre record of 122.448km/h (89.758mph) with the 500 M in the hands of Paul Péan. Never had a French 500cc reached such speeds! Of course, the figures were much less impressive for the standing-start kilometre, the lack of a gearbox being a severe handicap.

Ernest Henry's Peugeot career ended in catastrophe at the final pre-war race, at Fontainebleau, when the two Peugeots that had entered were forced to abandon with seized engines!

The Grémillon era

By the time the war was over, the team had broken up: Zuccarelli was killed during a test run in 1913, Boillot died in aerial combat in 1916 and Henry left for Ballot in 1919.

Marcel Grémillon, who succeeded to the Peugeot racing arm, hurriedly 'spruced up' the two-cylinder 500s by adding a three-speed gearbox with a kick-start taken from the production bikes, but retaining the reduction gearing. This version had its first outing at the Eure circuit, from 14 to 16 August 1919 with the same drivers (and Peugeot employees during the week): Paul Péan, Lionel Perrin and Lucien

Desvaux. But once again, the narrow, winding circuit didn't suit the big bikes: the perfidious Alcyon 350 got the better of Peugeot, finishing seven minutes ahead.

The Alcyon–Peugeot battle went a step further in August 1920, for the first real post-war track race. This time, Alcyon lined up its 500 V-twin (same dimensions, 62 x 82mm, as the Peugeot), while the Peugeot 500 gave an inaugural run to its third version. The DOHC drive was no longer central, but on the right-hand side of the cylinders, and there was now a full engine-block incorporating a three-speed gearbox, clutch and kick-start. Lubrication, the engine's weak point, had also been revised with a double pump and an impressive flexible-pipe system carrying oil to all the key points. But again, the three Peugeots had to abandon the race after breakdowns, and Alcyon took all the categories.

Victory finally came at the Côte de Gaillon races in the 750 category, followed by Gometz-le-Châtel where the Peugeots won a triple victory with Péan in the 500 and 700 categories, and Gillard in the 1,000cc climbing the 1,000m hill in a record-beating 35 $\frac{1}{5}$ seconds (an average speed of more than 122km/h [76mph]) on a bored-out 500, a performance that the Alcyons simply couldn't match. Gillard then went on to win the Lyon Grand Prix, but the DOHC Peugeots barely managed to distinguish themselves in the big races of 1921 and 1922. Their last battle came in March 1923 at the Côte du Camp race, where the 500 and 750cc bikes broke new records.

●●●● The Boulicot replica: Henry's rebirth

While one can criticise the cynical replicas that are passed off as originals, one can only salute the enthusiast who invests all his time and know-how in reviving a masterpiece of our heritage that has sadly disappeared. Thanks to a titanic effort, this monument to the history of French motorbikes lives again and was in action on the race tracks in 2010 for the first time in 96 years. The twin-cylinder, eight-valve Peugeot Grand Prix of 1913 has been fully recreated by Jean Boulicot, an electronics engineer by profession. 'In 2000 we found all the plans for the four-valve, twin-shaft 500s at the Peugeot Museum at Sochaux (or Valentigney, to be precise),' Jean explains. 'I simply had to reconstruct this masterpiece, choosing the easiest, the 1913 version with no gearbox. Over nearly ten years and some twenty-five thousand hours of work, assisted by two other people for the cycle part and the casting, I made everything at home from the plans, using a 1960 Ernault Batignolles lathe and a slightly younger Alcera milling machine!'

Paul Péan in 1919 at the Eure race track where he won in the 500cc category. This M1 modified for the first time by Grémillon is neither especially attractive nor well thought out with reduction gearing and a chain driving the three-speed box with a kick-start (from the production 750) and another chain to drive the wheel. Note that all the M1s up until 1922, like the present-day Harley-Davidsons, have two pairs of footrests for the driver's comfort.

The full Peugeot team on the start line at the Eure track in 1919. From left to right: Paul Péan and Lionel Perrin, respectively first and second in the 500cc category, and Lucien Desvaux about whom nothing is known other than that he was a Peugeot employee like the others.

The 1920 third version of the 500 M1 with the OHC drive on the right-hand side and a completely new engine-block incorporating a three-speed gearbox. Also new was the rear drum brake. Paul Péan is seen here at Gometz in 1920, where he would do the 1,000m hill-climb in 35.2 seconds, making a clean sweep of the 750 and 1,000cc categories.

1921: the fourth and final version of the DOHC, eight-valve 500 has lost its kick-start and received a bulky-looking dry clutch.

On the Day of Records at the Allée des Acacias in the Bois de Boulogne, Paul Péan covered the flying kilometre at 137.405km/h (85.382mph) on this 1921 M 500; a speed that would be both impossible and prohibited at the venue today.

At Le Mans in 1921, the third version of the DOHC Peugeot now has a gearbox but still only one flimsy drum brake on the back wheel.

Revolutionary as its design was, the eight-valve 500, already seven years old, was no longer competitive, and Peugeot took on a young Romanian engineer, Lessman Antonesco, a graduate of the Bucharest Industrial Art and Design School to replace Marcel Grémillon.

Antonesco retained only the general layout of the original two-cylinder bikes: the external flywheel on the left and the clutch unit on the right, and over the winter of 1922–1923 he worked on possible solutions for a new engine: double or single OHC, two or four valves per cylinder, operated by push rods, rocker arms or tappets. The only common thread in these plans was the shaft-and-bevel-gear OHC drive and a completely new engine-block horizontally split and incorporating a three-speed gearbox, solutions that were as up to date as they were unusual for the time. In the end he kept the simplest part of the concept: a 360° twin-cylinder engine with single OHC and two valves per cylinder.

The engine appeared to constitute a step backwards, but in fact it would turn out to be more consistently reliable than its predecessors, whose cylinder heads – with all their perforations – were chronically lacking in rigidity, lubrication and cooling... which are not exactly trivial problems! While the solution adopted may have seemed less bold, it quickly proved itself to be soundly based, with an output of 27hp at 5,200rpm (on an alcohol–benzene mixture) as well as great flexibility of use.

Built to be a winner

From the start, Paul Péan, René Gillard and the Marseillais Richard achieved wonders with the machine. Whether in big international events or in setting speed records, there were few accolades that were not heaped on them, despite the fierce competition from ABC, Alcyon, Douglas, Koehler-Escoffier, Norton and Sunbeam. They amassed a total of 21 victories in 23 races. No French motorbike since 1923 could boast such a fine international record.

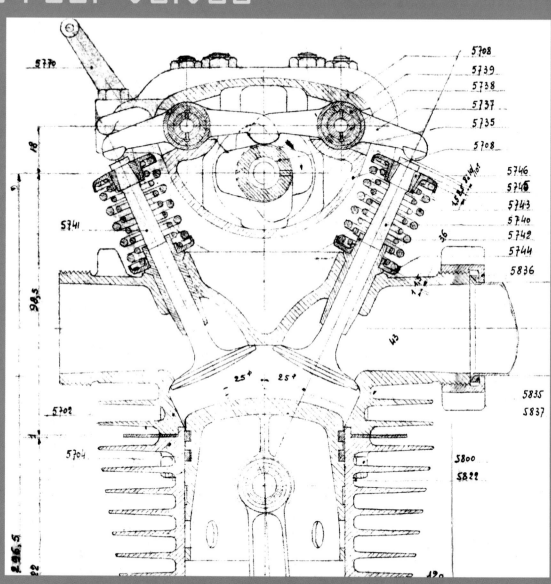

December 22, 1922 (model produced in 1924): Antonesco makes a wise decision with a plan for a modern and greatly simplified valve gear. A single OHC operates two valves via rockers. This was the solution ultimately adopted.

Especially memorable were Gillard's first win in the May 1923 Lyon Grand Prix, Péan's 157.9km/h (98.1mph) flying kilometre on 27 May 1923 at Nîmes, first, second and fourth places in the Swiss Grand Prix on 10 June, and above all the maker's hat-trick at the Monza Grand Prix des Nations on 8 September 1923: Gillard came first over the 400km at an average of 120.5m/h (74.9mph), Gremaud was second and Richard third out of 52 starters. Finally, on 29 September, Gillard won the Spanish Grand Prix, the inaugural race on the Sitges ring, at an average of 125km/h (77.7mph).

The season's only failure took place at the French Motorcycling Union's Grand Prix, where an epidemic of burnt-out valves on the three Peugeots in the race gave the win to Douglas.

Antonesco's 500 in its very first version, competing in the Lyon Grand Prix in May 1923. Gillard came in first in freezing rain and seven minutes ahead of the Alcyon, after covering 300km at an average of 95.012km/h (59.04mph).

Developments

The year 1924 saw a considerable development of the 500: it gained front brakes, exchanged its ordinary single-cradle frame for a well-made double cradle, its Druid fork for a Webb, which was very similar to the one on the competing Alcyons, abandoned its drip-feed lubrication system to strategic points with a pump to return it to the tank in favour of proper dry-sump lubrication with a mechanical pump and an oil reservoir in a casing under the engine.

After a further win at the Lyon Grand Prix, the Lion marque's 500s made little impression until the famous Isle of Man Tourist Trophy. Peugeot was given a tumultuous reception, as it was then a rare occasion for a big Continental manufacturer to line up for this prestigious race, although it is worth remembering that the Norton that won the first Tourist Trophy in 1907 used a Peugeot brothers' engine.

The Peugeot riders had just a few days to familiarise themselves with the circuit, so different from what they had known back home, but were at least able to do so under optimum conditions; Alec Bennett, winner of the 1922 Tourist Trophy, even made a test trip around the circuit with Gillard, pointing out the danger spots. There was great excitement at the start, with the Marseillaise being played before a hatless, standing crowd (quite different from today's football crowds!) and this was repeated at the finish, with Gillard's 11th place (out of 35 starters) being an excellent performance for someone new to the race. It also earned him a Tourist Trophy Replica for having finished within 10% of the winner's time. Other notable achievements that year were: two world records over the flying mile and flying kilometre broken by Péan at Arpajon on 6 July in the 750cc category (boring out the cylinders from 62 to 70mm brought the capacity up to 631cc), at a speed of over 165km/h (103mph). For this feat, a lightened M2 was used, with a return to the 1923 single-cradle frame. (On the same day, the Brough Superior driven by Le Vack, took the 1,000cc-category record in the same events to more than 191km/h [118mph]).

The competition was getting steadily stiffer and, apart from a few hill-climb wins, nothing of any significance was achieved in 1925. In 1926 it was hardly any better, despite second places for Gillard in the UMF Grand Prix and Péan in the French Grand Prix, followed by a first and second from Péan and Richard in the Lyon Grand Prix. In December 1926, Antonesco set about an in-depth updating of the machine, abandoning the 360° phasing of the crankshaft (English style, as it would later be described) in favour of 180° (like the Honda CB 250/350/450). But it was all too late and the new

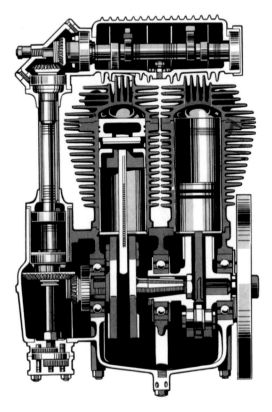

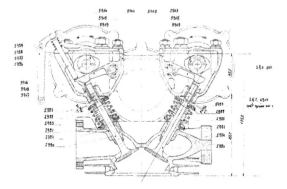

January 12, 1923: had Antonesco not yet made up his mind, or was he thinking of later giving the 500 a single OHC? This plan marks a return to a double overhead camshaft with four valves per cylinder operated by rocker arms.

December 3, 1926: the M2 500 is seen here with the crankshaft set at 180°. The cutaway unfortunately doesn't show whether Antonesco had envisaged twin-carburettor fuel supply, more logical with such a setting. The oil tank has left the engine casing and is back on the outside. This is the engine that would be discovered and rebuilt by Jean Nougier.

The superb cover drawing by Géo Ham for the Peugeot magazine in 1923 clearly shows the lubrication device of the early versions. A submerged oil pump ensured the return of the lubricant to the tank. Two drip-feed pumps on the right side of the tank provided lubricant as required to the camshaft (rear pump) and the crankshaft (front pump). Another pump on the left supplied an extra squirt if it was needed.

Above is seen the Peugeot equipage in the Spanish Grand Prix. Gillard, the winner of the 500 c.c. class at over 78 m.p.h., is standing on the extreme right, with hand on hip. He also won the 500 c.c. class of the Italian Grand Prix.

Even the English press couldn't praise this French motorbike highly enough! An extract from *Motor Cycling* in 1923 showing the Peugeot team at the Spanish Grand Prix, on the Sitges circuit.

engine almost certainly never raced. (Bought by Richard in 1927, then restored by Jean Nougier, it is the only surviving Peugeot twin-cylinder Grand Prix.)

A victim of the crisis

Things were going very wrong for Peugeot by 1926. The car sector, in serious trouble since 1924, got itself involved in some unwise activities, with the result that in March it was decided to separate the two sectors so that a bankruptcy in the car-making arm would not bring down the whole company.

Financially and policy-wise, the restructuring was not without consequences for the new Peugeot Cycles Company. In so far as the 500 had little connection with the kind of bikes that they were looking to sell (since 1922, Peugeot has produced only utility two-strokes), it would have to bear the cost of the current upheaval: with Antonesco's departure in 1927, its career was over, and the racing section closed in 1929. War and politics managed to kill these bikes, which in the 1910s and 1920s were the most advanced motorcycles produced in France – and perhaps the rest of the world too. Let's hope that the present-day rapprochement between Peugeot Motorcycles and Peugeot Automobiles will have a positive effect.

An unbeatable team in 1923 thanks to a motorbike that could reach 160km/h (100mph) and three keen drivers: from left to right, Gillard, Richard and Péan.

The 1923 Antonesco version with SOHC covered the flying kilometre at 166.44km/h (103.42mph) at Arpajon on 6 July, and Peugeot took the first two places in the French Grand Prix at Montlhéry with Richard (at an average of 141.69km/h [88mph] over 200km) ahead of Péan.

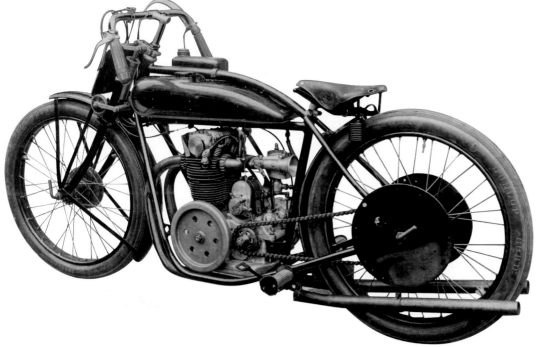

A new version of the M2 appeared at the 1924 Lyon Grand Prix, winning it brilliantly. The 1924 Tourist Trophy programme contained this magnificent three-quarter rear view, showing the new fuel tank with its rounded shape and topped by a small oil tank for direct lubrication of the OHC. The engine would henceforth include a mechanical pump located under the drive for the OHC control shaft and connected to a false three-litre sump under the engine. The fork has an enclosed central spring. Take a good look at the special Zénith carburettor and the handlebars which, on all versions, were attached to a bicycle-type bracket. The biggest difference in comparison with the other versions on this page is the double-cradle frame. (Yves Campion Archive)

Montlhéry, 1926 UMF Grand Prix: Peugeot entered four new versions of its M2. Big drum brake at the front, fuel tank under the saddle. The oil tank regains its place ahead of the rear wheel. Also note the protective plate in front of the exhaust-valve rockers. The felt and copper gaskets would not be sufficient to prevent oil getting on to the tyre without a mudguard! (Alain Chapeau Archive)

The 1926 Antonesco–Nougier 500 next to a single-cylinder 350 with SOHC of the same year. This 350, which almost certainly never officially raced, is of very similar construction to the 500 twin with shaft-driven OHC and an engine-block with a horizontal gasket. With the exception of the upper part of the engine, it's amazingly similar to Peugeot's star of the 1926 Salon, the 350 P 104 with engine-block and side valves designed by... Antonesco.

●●●● DOHC, eight-valve Henry 500 of 1913-1914 and Grémillon of 1918-1922

Four-stroke, twin-cylinder, in-line transverse, air-cooled phased at 360° – 496cc (62 x 82mm) – Integrally-cast cylinder and head with DOHC running in two sets of ball bearings – Steel piston – Tappet-operated valves – One-piece crankshaft on two bearings, cottered outside flywheel – Assembled connecting rod with white-metal bearings – Drip-feed lubrication for the OHC (hollow and provided with drips) and lubrication of the lower engine from a reservoir at the front; oil circulation by mechanical pump – Verified engine weight with the magneto but without the carburettor: 29kg – Longuemare, later Zénith carburettor – Single-cradle open frame, no front brake.

●●●● Henry 1913-1914

DOHC drive between the cylinders – Bigger oil pump on the final 1914 versions – Gear transmission to an intermediate shaft carrying the front pulley of the secondary belt transmission, valve gear and, underneath, the magneto drive – Block brakes on wheel rims at the rear.

●●●● Grémillon 1/1919

Similar, but geared primary transmission, secondary to a three-speed gearbox by chain no two, final by chain no three.

●●●● Grémillon 2/1920

Right-hand side DOHC gear drive – Three-speed engine block-gearbox, clutch and kick-start system in the engine casing – Drum brakes at the rear.

●●●● Grémillon 3/1921

Similar, but larger-diameter dry clutch in an open housing – No kick-start.

●●●● Antonesco SOHC, four-valve 500cc, 1923-1928

In-line, transverse, Four-stroke, twin-cylinder, air-cooled – 496cc (62 x 82mm) [Special versions for the 750 category (70 x 82 or 631cc) established a record flying kilometre of 172kph] – Engine/gearbox unit horizontally split – Bolted-up crankshaft on three sets of ball bearings, phased at 360° until December 1926, then at 180° on the final 1927 version restored by Jean Nougier – Monobloc connecting rods with big end on two sets of roller bearings and bushes at the little end – SOHC distribution on ball bearings, and driven by shaft and bevel gears, two valves per cylinder operated by rockers with coil-spring return – Compression ratio 5:4 at the time (alcohol), between

7 and 8 today (petrol) – 27hp at 5200rpm – Fed by a single Zénith special carburettor – Geared primary transmission and chain secondary – Multidisc dry clutch – Three-speed gearbox, right-hand operated – Drum brakes front and rear (no front brake in 1923) – Spindle hub at rear – 27in wheels (1923) then 26in (3.00 x 21 on the version restored by Nougier) – Between 100.6 and 114kg (empty, verified weight of the 500cc bikes at the UMF Grand Prix on the 24th June 1923) – Max. speed 166km/h (103mph).

●●●● 1923

Single-cradle open frame, no front brake and Druid-type parallelogram front fork with two lateral springs – Small drum brake at rear with internal shoes and external band.

●●●● 1924

New double-cradle frame (almost identical to the one used on the 1925 175 M and the 1926 P104 350), new Webb-type fork with a central spring – Small drum brake at the front – Oil tank no longer under the seat, but in a false sump under the engine with an extra small tank on top of the petrol tank.

●●●● 1925

Two-part petrol tank around the frame's top tube – Large front drum brake – Dry-sump lubrication – Oil tank is again separate, ahead of the frame's rear tube.

●●●● December 1926

Crankshaft phased at 180° – Trial use of hairpin valve-springs not ultimately retained – Various engine improvements.

The author in the saddle of the 1926 Peugeot 500 restored by Jean Nougier, on a ride up Mont Ventoux.

The 1927 single-cylinder 350 SOHC at the Coupes Moto Légende at Dijon in 2009.

Here's the proof. It is indeed a 180° configuration on this last 1927 version. (Jacky Bœuf)

Still with the same 175 Villiers TT engine, Allegro also raced in the sidecar category, as Tell Grandjean shows here in 1927 at Neuchâtel-Chaumont. (Bruno Badin Archive)

ALLEGRO (1925-1930)
A Swiss of substance

Allegro, in music, indicates a brisk, lively rhythm, and was the name Arnold Grandjean applied to his range of bicycles and later motorcycles that would sweep the board in Swiss hill-climbing races between 1925 and 1930.

However, it is claimed that the name's real origin was simply a phonetic rendering of 'Allez, gros! Allez! (Come on fat man! Come on!) that keen supporters of the great cyclist Arnold Grandjean shouted to encourage the rather portly star. Whatever the truth, Arnold, who was not lacking a sense of humour, gave this name to the cycle firm he set up in 1914 with his brothers Jules and Ali.

Arnold, whose first cycling success was in 1908 when he was 18, became the Swiss Champion in 1910 and began building his first bicycles under the Allegro name in 1914. In 1916, Arnold, young Ulysse and Tell Grandjean, along with the racing motorcyclist Marcel Bourquin opened new workshops and showrooms at Neuchâtel, where the first Allegro motorcycles were built in 1923. With these four in the driving seat, the 175cc Allegros with British Villiers Brooklands engines soon began to make an impression on the circuits with 14 national titles between 1925 and 1937 (six of which were won by Bourquin). From Klausen to the Col de Bruch via Nyon/Saint-Cergues, Arnold, Tell and especially Marcel Bourquin amassed 94 wins in their hill-climbing category and took some 66 national records, from Basel to Geneva and Zurich, in the very popular flying kilometre races. Allegro, the 175cc Swiss Champion from 1925 to 1929, managed an extraordinary performance in the 1928 European Grand Prix by being the only manufacturer to have all the machines it entered finish the race, and this at an average of more than 90km/h (56mph).

Driving his 175cc Allegro, Marcel Bourquin beat the Swiss record at Nyon/Saint-Cergues in 1927. It might be called road racing, but looking at the state of the course, might it better be called enduro? (Bruno Badin Archive)

A return to its beginnings for this 1928 Allegro 350 caught at the first Klausen hill-climb retrospective in 1993.

Encouraged by these successes, Tell Grandjean built a special 350cc in 1929, based around two 172cc Villiers Brooklands engines linked in tandem and shoehorned into a raised and greatly strengthened frame along with a standard Druid fork likewise treated. The 350 achieved some remarkable times in hill-climb races according to newspaper reports of the time, adding still more laurels to its crown.

Racing isn't everything, of course, and like the good managers they were, the Grandjean brothers took full advantage of their amazing success to sell their standard Allegro models. Production began with two-stroke bikes, using 147cc Villiers engines, followed in 1925 by 247 and 342cc models and, not unexpectedly, a Super-Sport version powered by the same 175cc Villiers Brooklands so successfully used in the Monet-Goyons driven by Sourdot and Homaire. The range expanded in 1929 with only the 172 and 342cc Villiers models remaining, but now joined by four-stroke machines powered by Sturmey Archer engines OHV or SV, in 348 and 496cc versions. In late 1932, the 350 and 500 four-strokes exchanged their English engines for Swiss Mag engines, and the 500 had a claimed output of 20hp at 4,500rpm. In the immediate post-war period, a Villiers-powered 125 appeared in the firm's advertising, but it was never put on sale. The company restarted production with Villiers 175 and 200cc bikes, and a final 1956 model built only in very limited numbers had a Belgian Gillet two-stroke 250cc engine.

ALLEGRO

ETABLISSEMENTS DES CYCLES ET MOTOCYCLETTES ALLEGRO
ARNOLD GRANDJEAN, NEUCHATEL (SUISSE)

Ali Grandjean
Zweiter Preis Neuchâtel-Chaumont
Kat. 175em3 Experten auf «Allegro».

Allegro or 'Allez, gros'? Ali Grandjean, featured on this 1926 catalogue, celebrated a second place in the Expert 175cc category at Neuchâtel-Chaumont.

Renowned for their great reliability, Villiers engines were used by many firms in Britain, France, Switzerland and Belgium. This 350 was nevertheless less common than the 147, 175 and 250cc engines. (Bruno Badin Archive)

March 1929. Photographed outside the company's factory in the Avenue de la Gare, Neuchâtel, these two Allegro 350s, with heavy sidecars attached, are setting out on a 'five continents' expedition, although it is unknown whether the expedition actually took place! (Bruno Badin Archive)

Tell Grandjean in 1927 in Zurich, where he had just broken the Swiss 175cc-category, flying-kilometre record, with 118km/h (73mph). (Bruno Badin Archive)

Tell Grandjean posing proudly in 1939 with his amazing twin-engine 350 fed by two Amal 15 MDYs with lateral air regulators. To say the least, the reinforcements to the frame and production fork were not done for reasons of style, and the consequent raising of the frame without moving the mudguards makes the wheels look too small. Note the separate lubrication device! (Bruno Badin Archive)

The firm's lapel badge.

Family photo: from left to right, Marcel Bourquin, Tell and Ulysse Grandjean, and two other Allegro drivers. (Bruno Badin Archive)

The August 1931 Swiss Grand Prix. Marcel Bourquin on a 175cc Allegro leads a Puch of the same cylinder capacity. (Bruno Badin Archive)

Allegro's advertising was inevitably concerned with competition as is shown here in 1933 by these two 500cc bikes with Sturmey Archer engines, which had just taken part in the Paris–Les Pyrénées–Paris and Liège–Milan–Liège rallies. (Bruno Badin Archive)

Marcel Bourquin on his Allegro 175 Brooklands in 1928. (Bruno Badin Archive)

●●●● Details of the 1925 Allegro models with Villiers engines

● **Cubic capacity** (cc)	172	147	247	342
● **Performance** (hp/rpm)	7/3,500	4/3,500	5/3,000	6/3,000
● **Weight** (kg)	72	60	80	90
● **Speed** (kph)	85	60	70	75

This 125 announced after the war is known only from the catalogue, but was almost certainly never produced.

N owadays, we swear by Japanese technology, yet most of it dates from long ago and was invented in places such as Germany, Italy... and Belgium.

A four-cylinder pioneer since 1904, FN stopped producing them in 1926 and did not return to multi-cylinder types until 1937 with the M12 flat twin (designed to be attached to huge driven-wheel sidecars for the Army) and the highly original M14 unveiled in July of the same year at the Belgian Grand Prix in Spa. This vertical two-cylinder bike with its light-alloy engine-block and Roots supercharger was to take over from the single-cylinder OHC 500, which was losing its competitive edge when up against the Nortons, DOHC Saroléas and other multi-cylindered bikes that were popping up on the Grand Prix circuit. The substantial engine-block, as on all the products of this manufacturer, was distinguished by its valve train system, which, to my knowledge, is the only one of its type. Cylinders and cylinder heads were separate and each head had its own chain-driven SOHC. Apart from this highly complex arrangement, whose only raison d'être seems to have been that parts from the single-cylinder M86 could be reused, the engine was of a thoroughly modern design compared with the archetype of twin-cylinder machines on the road, the 500cc Triumph Speed Twin, which appeared the same year. The magnesium crankcases were cast in Paris. Another up-to-date feature of the engine-block was its five-speed gearbox (in fact four speeds and an overdrive) that had already been used on the record-breaking single-cylinder models.

Fast but fragile

The fine-looking M14 would unfortunately have a very short career. It made a poor start at the July 1937 Belgian Grand Prix, where René Milhoux dropped out with a damaged gearbox.

Milhoux then managed to convince the FN factory to get a 600cc version ready to make an attempt on the sidecar speed records. This engine capacity was allowed until 1950 when the rules were changed to come into line with solo bikes, with a maximum capacity of 500cc.

The bore was increased from 60 to 65mm and, fed by the Roots supercharger, the power output went up to 60hp at 6,000rpm. The single-cradle frame, still without rear suspension, was lowered and lengthened, and attached to an ultra-streamlined sidecar weighted with a 65kg sand bag in accordance with the rules. The unit weighed 252kg and had a maximum speed of 177kph. It won its first honours on 28 October 1937 on the Montlhéry circuit. Milhoux and Charlier gained four sidecar world records in the process,

This second version has been completely revised: oval-tube frame with cantilever rear suspension on rubber rings, oil tank moved from the rear left of the frame to in front of the engine, new carburettor with a very long feed pipe. (Sulz Museum, Erich and Marion Waldmann Collection)

A superb, compact engine-block, even with the OHC drive on each side of the cylinders. The rockers are totally enclosed and they can be adjusted from the outside.

including 50km at an average of 156.616kph and 50 miles at an average of 157.367kph, which would not be beaten for a further 12 years.

FN now turned increasingly to the growing discipline of motocross. The M14 reappeared sporadically during 1938 and 1939, this time with rear cantilever suspension and rubber rings, a RN carb replacing the TT, a new Marshall-Roots supercharger and the oil radiator in front of the engine. In this form, it achieved a few good results in the Coupes de la Meuse, Coupes de l'Armistice, Schaerbeek 24 Hours and Paris–Nice, among others, as well as gaining its best international placing in July 1939 in the European Grand Prix at Spa-Francorchamps, with Ginger Woods coming fourth at an average of 142kph. A final version appeared briefly in 1939 with a new frame, a stronger, 6cm-wider engine and twin carburettors.

Fed on a petrol–benzene mixture through a Roots supercharger, the M14 develops 46hp at 6,200rpm and can reach 200kph. This 1937 model, the record-breaking 600cc, develops 60hp and can reach 177kph with a sidecar!

Chimay, 1998: René Milhoux, FN's official driver, is overcome at being reunited with his machine.

The second-version FN M14, in the period and after a magnificent restoration.

●●●● **1937 M14**

Four-stroke, twin-cylinder, air-cooled – 498cc (60 x 88mm) – 48hp at 6,200rpm (on petrol–alcohol) – 584cc (65 x 88mm) and 60hp at 6,000rpm – Two chain-driven SOHC and two valves per cylinder – Compression 5.2 to 8.6 – Roots supercharger and a single carburettor – Dry-sump lubrication – Five-speed gearbox – Multidisc dry clutch – Chain transmission – Single-cradle divided frame – Parallelogram front suspension – Drum brakes – Front tyres 3.00 x 21in, rear 4.00 x 19in – 174kg – 200kph.

The DKW Gegenläufer ('opposed runner') reappeared in the 1970s, but it was not until 1991 that it was running properly after an expert restoration conducted by the University of Darmstadt.

DKW US 250 GEGENLÄUFER (1949)
Four pistons in two cylinders

After the war, Russian troops discovered plans in DKW's Zschopau plant for an astonishing 250 and 350cc racing bike with two cylinders, four opposed pistons and a rotary supercharger.

The Belgian Laguesse machines featured earlier in this book were essentially quite simple in comparison with this DKW 250 designed to reap a harvest of victories for Hitler's Germany. The 'Gegenläufer', as the Germans named it, was first heard about in 1938. The layout was unique and highly original, with a crankshaft at each end of the two cylinders arranged transversally in the pressed-metal frame, and two pistons in each cylinder. The two crankshafts were linked by a gear train, the gearbox was incorporated in the engine-block and it had a shaft drive secondary transmission. The bore was 33.5mm and the stroke 34.7mm for each piston, to give 69.35mm. A central supercharger fed the lot, and this early version developed 35hp at 6,000rpm.

In 1939, power output was increased to 39.5hp and, when fed on a petrol–alcohol mixture, it reached 48.5hp.

Keen to break records themselves, the Russians, in control of eastern Germany where the Zschopau factory was located, decide to halt development: Army Major Koganov then took charge of putting together a team composed of DKW racing specialists, with engineers Kurt Bang and Karl Kluge working on the engine, Manfred Lohse on the frame, and Friedrich, the engineer who had worked during the war on the supercharged DKW SS 250 and 350, as well as Siegfried Wünsche, the former factory rider. The head of the team was none other than Obering, the former boss of DKW's racing arm.

Despite its substantial appearance, this 250cc bike weighs just 150kg!

The Gegenläufer 250 developed behind the Iron Curtain in 1946. The engine was arranged transversally at this time.

A truly complex piece of engineering.

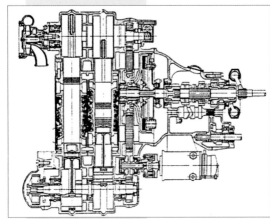

From 1946 to the end of 1948, there were only four 350cc and one 250cc Gegenläufers built, with the latter's dimensions increasing to 35 x 64mm and the supercharger supply pressure going to 11.5 bars. Unlike on the surviving restored example, the engines were arranged crossways in the pressed-steel frames. The gearbox was built in and it had a shaft drive transmission. Once the bikes were completed, they were carefully packed into cases and sent east... never to return!

Racing machines frequently turn up by some miracle, years after disappearing. So it happened that a 250cc engine, built secretly in the east, arrived in the west via a private DKW racer, Kurt Kuhnke. Having completed their work for the Russians, the previously mentioned development team was engaged by Kuhnke and they fitted the engine into a pre-war cycle part. This time it was arranged lengthways, with a separate gearbox under the rear crankshaft. It created a sensation in post-war German racing, up until the banning of superchargers in 1951, when it disappeared... to surface once again in the mid-1970s, a collector entrusting the University of Darmstadt with the task of reconstructing a complete motorbike using the surviving parts. The result surpassed the original, with power output now up to 65hp at 8,500rpm. Not bad for a 250cc weighing 150kg!

In all my years on the circuits, I've never heard such a noisy engine. Look at the spectators' reactions!

●●●● **1949 US 250**
Two-stroke, twin-cylinder, liquid-cooled engine – Four opposed pistons and two crankshafts connected by a gear train – 245cc (33.5 x 69.35mm) – 1946–1949 prototype: 45.5hp at 7,000rpm – Separate, foot-operated, four-speed gearbox – Chain transmission – Double-cradle frame – Telescopic front and rear suspension – 21in tyres – 150kg – 180km/h (112mph).

The year 1953 was a turning point: the famous Norton Manx had to give up its last hope of being once again the world champion. The four-cylinder Gilera 500s and NSU and Moto Guzzi 250s and 350s were dominating their respective categories. Doug Hele of BSA (later to head up Norton and BSA-Triumph racing departments) was in great secrecy, designing an extraordinary 250 that it was hoped would restore British manufacturers to the winner's podium. Sadly, events were to take a different course.

BSA MC1 250 (1954)
Hopes dashed

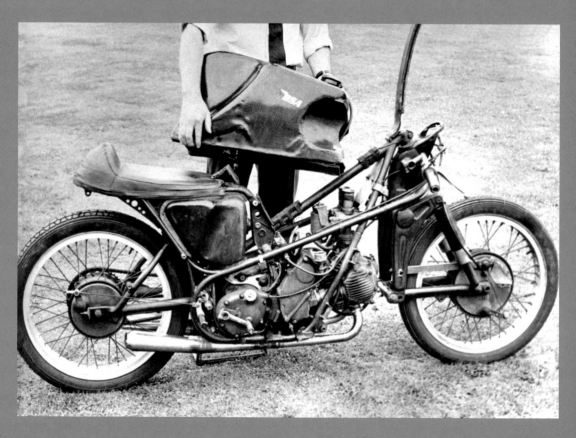

The very modern chassis that proved to be particularly stiff. Geoff Duke's only criticism concerned the front brake.

The BSA 250 racing bike designed to take over the baton from the Norton Manx 350 that had slipped behind the NSUs and Moto Guzzis was conceived in BSA's special workshops in early 1953 by Doug Hele, overseen by his boss Bert Hopwood.

The extraordinarily engineered horizontal monocylinder bike featured a valve train system that was as complex as it was novel. Four radial valves were operated by rockers from two half-OHCs. The right-hand OHC was driven by a shaft and bevel gears and linked to the left-hand half-OHC by a second set of bevel gears. Low-slung and compact, the MC1 also had a very up-to-date frame consisting of lower and upper double cradles with very straight tubes that crossed behind the steering column to support the front suspension.

Geoff Duke is impressed

Who better than Geoff Duke to give advice on the MC1's development? Even though he had by then signed for Gilera, winning the world 500cc title for them in 1953, 1954 and 1955, Duke, who had already been three times world champion on Norton 350 and 500cc bikes in 1951 and on the 350cc in 1952, was excited by Doug Hele and Bert Hopwood's plans, and closely followed the prototype's development, while also keeping the BSA team up to date with the progress being made by NSU.

In late 1954, he did 30-odd laps at Oulton Park, beating the 250cc lap record set by Cecil Sandford on a streamlined Mondial. His comments were enthusiastic: 'It's a superior machine to the Manx 350 and has the potential to take the

world title from the all-conquering Moto Guzzis and NSUs.'

The MC1 put out 35hp, an exceptional figure for the time, and had a maximum rpm of 10,000. Unstreamlined for the initial tests, it ran at 9,800rpm in fourth. However, not everything was yet quite right. An over-permeable valve timing (too much overlap of the valves) hampering compression at low revs made it difficult to start. A pair of stoppers had to be put in the exhaust pipes and Geoff Duke would remove them once the engine was running.

Nonetheless, the MC1 proved to be very fast, despite the need for improved fuel system performance and resonance in the exhaust: the engine would run only between 8,000 and 11,000rpm. Geoff Duke complained particularly about the separate four-speed gearbox that he thought should be

Low-slung, lightweight and faster, the MC1 would have been able to hold its own against the Moto Guzzis and NSU 250s, and even to take its place in the 350cc category to replace the Norton Manx. (Sammy Miller Museum)

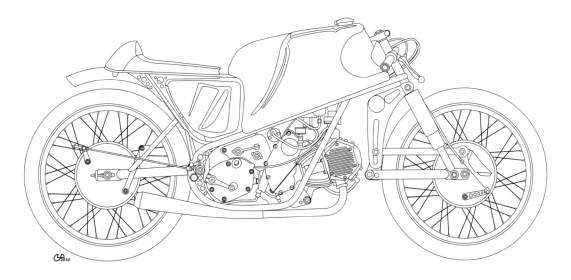

An extremely compact and modern motorbike.
(Drawing by Yves Campion)

At auction in the late 1950s.

When I met Doug Hele (far left) in 1984, he drew me a sketch of the valve arrangement on a corner of the tablecloth... Quite clear, wouldn't you say?

replaced by an integral five-speed box, which would extract more from an engine with such high revs, and about the front double-cam, full-width brake that he found poor. By contrast, the cycle parts were entirely satisfactory.

Win, or give up

It was agreed that Geoff Duke could take part in the next international race to be held at Silverstone in 1954, with the MC1 being rechristened Rudge for the occasion. So confident was Geoff Duke that he even sent in his entry for the next Tourist Trophy under the name of GDS (Geoff Duke Special) so as not to reveal BSA's involvement.

Despite its remarkable potential, the MC1 would never actually race. It was entered for Silverstone, but at the very

last moment, the BSA directors got cold feet and called a meeting with Doug Hele and demanded assurance of a win. With no answer to such an absurd question, it was decided to pull out.

BSA then abandoned the tests, fearful that the MC1 would not last the course. The Silverstone race was won by John Surtees on a NSU Sportmax of just 28hp!

After languishing a long time in the dusty corners where prototypes are consigned, the BSA MC1 is now part of Sammy Miller's fabulous collection, an absolute must-see if you're in the south of England (Sammy Miller Museum: www.sammymiller.co.uk).

●●●● Four-stroke, single-cylinder, air-cooled – 250cc – 35hp at 8500rpm – Two shaft-driven, half-OHC and four radial valves – Compression 10.5 – Two vertical carburettors – Dry sump – Four-speed, later five-speed separate gearbox – Tubed truss frame – Leading-link front suspension from pressed sheet and tubes, rear swing cantilever with horizontal damper – Drum brakes – 31-litre tank – 109kg.

NORTON AND THE MINI-MANXES

Records broken at Montlhéry, 1953. The tank is being filled while Ray Amm searches the skies.

I n the mid-1950s, the famous type 30 and 40 Manxes, while always in a majority on the 350 and 500cc circuits, were nonetheless being beaten by their Italian competitors. Norton made three attempts to give their big single-cylinder bikes a second wind... by shrinking them.

Kneeler (1953)
The Manx on its knees

The first came in 1953 with the well-known Silver Fish 350, soon nicknamed 'Kneeler', on which Ray Amm and Eric Oliver would set a number of world speed records at Montlhéry. The multi-cylinder Gileras dominated 500cc-category Grand Prix racing from 1952, along with the Moto Guzzi single-cylinder, DOHC 350, the world champion from 1953 to 1957. Having been the world champion manufacturer in 350cc bikes in 1951 and 1952, and in 500cc bikes in 1950 and 1951, Norton was keen to hit back. Without the means to develop its ambitious plans for a four-cylinder, liquid-cooled bike, the old Bracebridge Street factory in Birmingham, as usual, tried to make something new from something old.

Down on their knees

Norton designed a radically new bike around its old, but magnificent single-cylinder machine. Yet its genuflection before the multi-cylinder bikes was not merely figurative. So as to reduce the front surface area, it was driven in a kneeling position as with the lowered sidecar outfits fitted with small wheels that also appeared in the 1950s.

The first sidecar attachment of this type, built by the Swiss champion Hans Haldemann and Jost Albisser, actually appeared in 1950, and Eric Oliver raced such a Norton sidecar very much inspired by the Kneeler. The experiment

wasn't followed up, and this strange racer took part in just one competition, but a number of technical features that were tested would prove their value in later years.

Jointly developed by Norton in Birmingham, Artie Bell, the McCandless brothers and the Short Aircraft Company of Belfast, the Silver Fish carried out its first secret tests in March 1953 at Montlhéry and on the Isle of Man under Ray Amm and Ken Kavanagh.

This heavily clad Norton retained its conventional engineering but the driver's kneeling position and its streamlining gave it a revolutionary aerodynamic appearance.

The Works 350 engine was modified for the purpose with, among other things, a mechanical pump driven by the inlet camshaft and feeding the carburettor that was located higher up than the tank. By contrast, the innovative cycle part was completely new. Only the lower tubes and the steering head were retained. The two lowered upper tubes

held the cylinder head and were extended rearwards in a sort of lattice that supported the shock absorbers. Two long side tanks were fitted each side of the lower part of the engine and their twisted shape acted as a support for the driver's knees and elbows. The centre of gravity was consequently much lowered.

33 records at Montlhéry

This extraordinary machine's proper race debut took place at the North West 200 in May 1953 with the great Ray Amm driving. The Kneeler managed only three laps before being retired with carburation problems, but not before it had broken the lap record. For a while, that was its only race, but it was back on the track on 8 and 9 November 1953 at the Montlhéry circuit where it took 33 world records, including the all-categories hour at 215.2km/h (133.72mph) – better than the record set by Taruffi's supercharged Gilera 4 in 1939!

November 1953: Ray Amm takes 33 records on the Montlhéry banking.

Some 44 years after its exploits, the Silver Fish returns to Montlhéry with Sammy Miller at the 1997 Coupes Moto Légende. (Sammy Miller Museum)

Not so easy is it, Mr Miller, to push your bike when the saddle is so low! (Sammy Miller Museum)

●●●● 1953 Norton Kneeler 350
Four-stroke, single-cylinder, air-cooled – 350cc – Shaft driven DOHC – Two valves – Aluminium cylinder and head – Magneto ignition – Separate four-speed gearbox – Chain transmission – Lateral-construction, double-cradle frame – Telescopic front suspension and swingarm rear with two shock absorbers – Aluminium streamlining – Side fuel tanks – 19in wheels – 215kph.

All you have to do is lift the saddle to gain direct access to the top of the engine. (Sammy Miller Museum)

Streamlining everywhere... and a very odd vertical position for the brake and gear pedals! (Sammy Miller Museum)

The 'flat Manx' was never completed. A pity, as it would have been good to see Norton fight back against Italian industry using its own methods. (Sammy Miller Museum)

Model F (1955)
The Flat Manx

After the kneeling Manx, there was the flat Manx, inspired by the famous DOHC Guzzi 350, the world champion from 1953 to 1957.

The Norton Manx 350cc was more powerful but slower than the Moto Guzzi 350cc designed by the engineer Carcano, so Norton again worked on its aerodynamics. After the unprofitable experience with the Kneeler, the company's manager Joe Graig commissioned Ernie Walsh, an expert engineer from Vincent Motorcycles, to create from start to finish this unusual horizontal-cylinder Manx prototype. Unfortunately, the project really came too late, the single-cylinder engine being outdated by this time, and Norton decided to end any official participation in Grand Prix racing before they had even completed this, in many ways, interesting prototype.

A change of position for the engine

On this new model F (for 'flat'), under development from 1954 to 1956, the considerably modified 350cc engine was turned forwards through 90°, Moto Guzzi fashion. Identical in power to the standard vertical Manx, but with a smaller frontal surface area and a lowered centre of gravity, the new engine looked promising, but unfortunately the factory decided that its special bikes should have the same layout as the bikes sold to private individuals, and the 350 F never raced. Yet despite the British having a reputation for being traditionalists, the fact is that they have always been a nation of innovators. It is just this inventive, eccentric side that allowed the industry to survive in Britain. An excellent example of this is the Norton Commando, a brilliant and cheap concoction from an obsolete engine successfully adapted to fit into new cycle parts. While the horizontal-engine Manx may have been part of this same ingenious tradition, it was not to have the same happy outcome.

A comparison between the prototypes restored by Sammy Miller and John Surtees reveals numerous differences, both in the engine and the cycle parts. (John Surtees Collection)

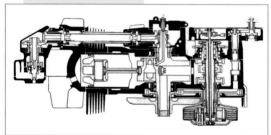

A cutaway of the 350 F's engine-block. The gearbox is tiny.

●●●● Four-stroke, single-cylinder, air-cooled – 348cc (71 x 88mm) – Shaft-driven DOHC, two valves – Special Amal GP carb, 36.5mm dia. – Dry-sump lubrication – Magneto ignition – Five-speed gearbox-engine – Dry clutch – Monotube girder frame – Front telescopic suspension and swing at rear – Twin-cam 200mm dia. drum brakes – 19in wheels.

The engine has been completely revised with a block and a five-speed gearbox. The cylinder head now has radial fins. (Sammy Miller Museum)

The carburettor fits into the U of the tank. (Sammy Miller Museum)

A Manx with an engine-block

To create such a remarkably compact bike, Norton had not been content merely to lay the engine flat, but had taken the opportunity to radically alter the design. To keep the wheelbase from being too long, the F was built using an engine/gearbox unit with, unusually for the time, an external flywheel, which allowed the crankcase to be made smaller while doing away with mixing of the engine oil by the flywheel. The crankcase was made from magnesium alloy and the geared primary transmission drove a new type of five-speed gearbox. Again, in an effort to reduce the size, it was not possible to use the famous Featherbed frame, and the cycle parts were reduced to their simplest form with a single upper tube, as on Eglis and Aermacchis, acting as an oil reservoir and topped off with a huge fuel tank. The engine was suspended at the front by two thin tubes and the Manx F must have held the record for the lowest centre of gravity.

This other factory prototype of the Norton 350 F was rebuilt in 1998 by the racing champion John Surtees. (John Surtees Collection)

Maximum compactness. The small flywheel and the dry clutch are on the outside. (Sammy Miller Museum)

Low Boy (1960)
The shrunken Manx

In 1960, in a final burst of energy, Doug Hele, Norton's great racing boss who already had to his credit the BSA 250 MC1, decided to make a top-to-bottom revision of the glorious Norton works racer.

There was virtually no change to the engine that had been designed for the Kneeler in 1953 and the Model F in 1955, and Doug Hele was principally concerned to lower the single's height and reduce the front surface area.

Whoops, we've shrunk the Manx!

There were no half measures here: the distorted fuel tank went under the seat and behind the cylinder, and a fuel pump driven by the admission camshaft sent fuel to a mini-tank underneath that was attached to the separate carburettor reservoir. The oil tank was located behind the gearbox, which required modifying and lengthening the rear part of the Featherbed frame and the swingarm fixing point. With this layout, the poor driver who would have had his chin just above the DOHC housing could see only the upper triple clamp of the fork. No problem: Doug Hele would get rid of the intrusive triple clamp – as he had already done on his 1952–1953 BSA 250 MC1 – shorten the fork tubes and weld them directly to a robust lower triple clamp turning on a 7.6cm-diameter bearing! The poor driver was left looking at the indispensable steering head. Compactness being of the essence, the centrally placed exhaust passed under the engine and had its outlet barely 18cm from the rear wheel.

A bike without support

The great Tourist Trophy specialist, Eddie Crooks, tested the Low Boy on the Isle of Man, during the 1960 Tourist Trophy

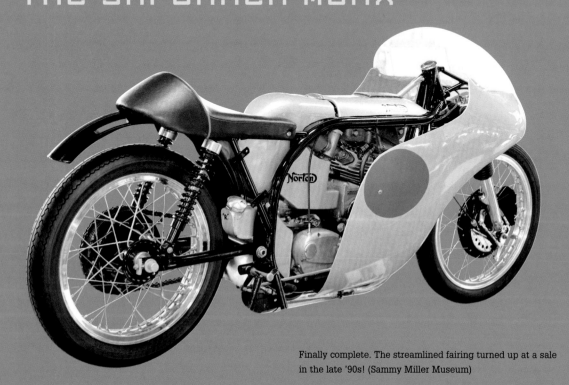

Finally complete. The streamlined fairing turned up at a sale in the late '90s! (Sammy Miller Museum)

With the steering head as a datum point and your chin resting on the tank, driving the Low Boy was, it would seem, an exhausting experience. (Sammy Miller Museum)

Good heavens, who shrunk the Manx? (Sammy Miller Museum)

●●●● **Norton Low Boy 350**
Standard Norton Manx 350 engine (76 x 76.7mm) – Shaft –driven DOHC and two valves with hairpin springs – Amal GP carb – Magneto ignition – Approx. 35hp at 7,200rpm – Separate five-speed gearbox – Chain primary and secondary transmission – Featherbed double-cradle frame – Telescopic front suspension and swing at rear – 19in front wheels, 18in rear – Twin-cam 178mm dia. brakes, single-cam at rear – Footrests positioned well back – Approx. 142kg and 195km/h (120mph).

trials and was not greatly impressed. He had to take much of his weight on his wrists and with no fuel tank to lie along he was unable to get low enough to take full advantage of the low profile of the machine. The tests lasted just one lap! After that, further tests were carried out at Oulton Park in October, following which the prototype, now fitted with a driver's 'chin-rest', was tried out in December 1960 by Phil Read. But the days of this final big mono were numbered, and Norton began to concentrate on its new twin-cylinder Dominator 500. The Low Boy missed scrapping by a hair's breadth, but Bob Collier, who worked in Norton's research and development department, saved what was left of the machine in 1962 when the old Birmingham factory was closed, and donated it to Sammy Miller for his museum. After six long years of restoration, the Low Boy made its first reappearance in the May 2000 Coupes Moto Légende.

However, its special polyester streamlining had gone missing. By sheer chance, about three or four years ago, an enthusiast discovered it on sale in Stafford in its original condition, with the number 11 that had been used on its only appearance in the Tourist Trophy trials in 1960. So, 48 years after being thrown out, the Low Boy is finally complete and on display at the Sammy Miller Museum.

A head-on view. No room for the race numbers! (Sammy Miller Museum)

1,000cc Seal Family Four, Great Britain 1924.
(Drawing by Yves Campion)

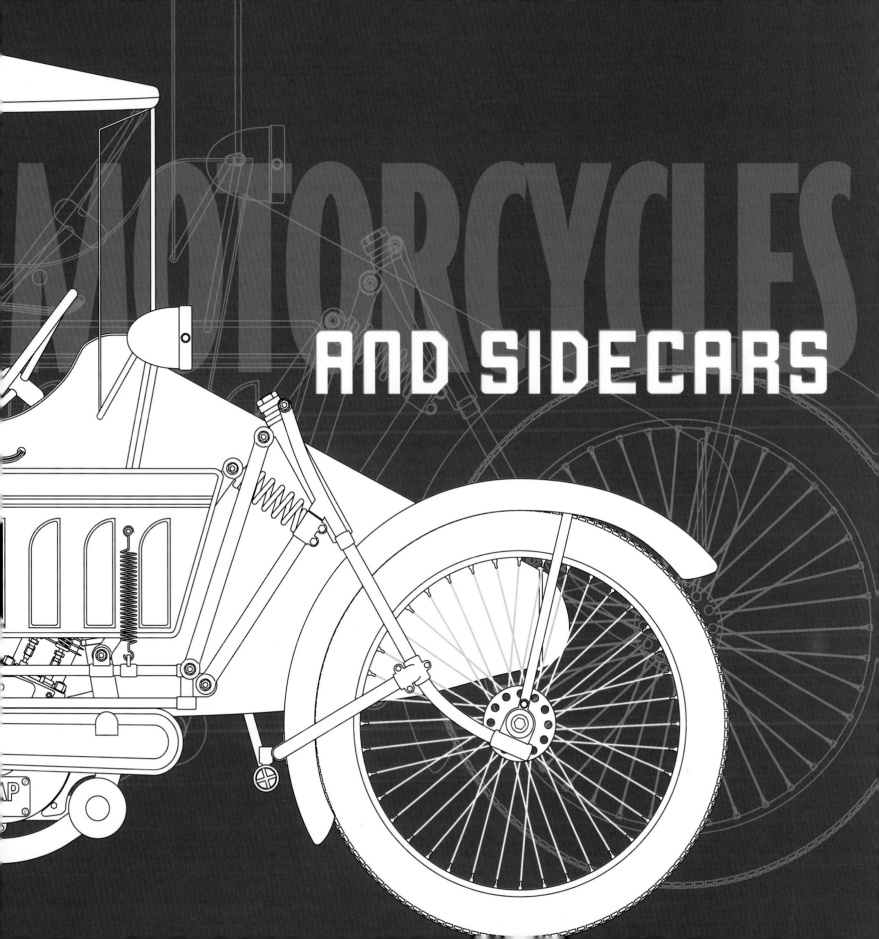

MOTORCYCLES

AND SIDECARS

MECCANO MOTORCYCLE AND SIDECAR (1928)
Going back in time

With remarkable authenticity, this superb model is entirely constructed from 1920s Meccano parts.

I am sure you will agree that our taste for old things is not inspired merely by an interest in history and the fine things that were created in the former times. We also enjoy the more personal journey of going back to our own past, the motorcycles of our youth, those of our parents, or recalling the motorcycling uncle or grandfather. So let's go back a little in time to that golden age when we first started making things.

The 1928 instructions.

How many of us have not experienced the delight of finding a Meccano set under the Christmas tree? We might have started off building a house, then a crane or a cable car and then, with a great deal of patience and a full set of parts from various sets, a motorbike and sidecar like the one available from Meccano France in the late 1920s. The excellent instructions (no 3 of 1928) precisely describe the construction, using 151 parts for the bike and 141 for the sidecar, with the bonus of a brief but clear technical history of the motorbike. The only item not provided by the famous manufacturer was the elastic band used for the primary transmission. Everything else came from Meccano's various sets and it all worked, apart from the two-cylinder V engine. The sidecar's body even had suspension.

The motorcycle and sidecar was for a long time the only economical alternative to the car, but the poor motorcyclist was left out in the rain! The solution is both logical and eccentric: put the driver in the sidecar...

SEAL FAMILY FOUR (1924)
Mad or logical?

The British often waver between extreme conservatism and the wildest futuristic imaginings, and surely only they would come up with such disconcerting logic: the only way to protect the driver from the elements is to put him in the sidecar! Conceived in 1912, the Seal appears to be the first example of its kind, followed eight years later by a much more sophisticated 'asymmetric three-wheeled vehicle', the Scott Sociable. With the word 'seal' covering both the marine animal and the idea of a protective element, there has been speculation about whether J. Haynes and C.A. Bradshaw (not to be confused with Granville Bradshaw, the celebrated engineer who designed, among others, the ABC motorcycles) actually intended this double meaning when they designed their strange hybrid vehicle.

No driver, no saddle, no handlebars

Getting together in 1906 to build bicycles, Haynes and Bradshaw soon began to think about making three- and four-wheeled motorised vehicles. Named the 'Seal', an acronym for 'safe, economical and light', their first vehicle with the driver in the sidecar was exhibited at the 1912 London Show. The most phlegmatic of English gentlemen must have dropped their bowlers and umbrellas in astonishment on seeing this extraordinary machine, powered by a 770cc, side-valve, V-twin JAP engine, whose driver sat in the sidecar next to his passenger and steered using a 'cow's tail' ie a single arm.

In 1914, the engine size went up from 770cc to 980cc, the rear-hub gears were replaced with a conventional three-speed box, the belt gave way to a chain, the 'cow's tail' became a steering wheel and it gained a kick-starter. In 1918, the wheels were made interchangeable, with quickly detachable features, and the sidecar gained a spare. Two years later, the company gave up the name of Haynes and Bradshaw, replacing it with the Seal brand. The chassis was redesigned, shaft transmission was adopted, along with a gearbox having two forward and two reverse gears and a coned clutch working in oil. The engine was now concealed in a casing. Unfortunately, the 2 x 2-speed gearbox turned

Not only rare but expensive, the four-seater Seal Family Four cost £138 in 1924, at a time when the most luxurious motorbike and sidecar, the 8hp AJS, cost only £115.

The top of the steering head is pivoted and, lower down, a swingarm is controlled by a spring.

1924 Seal Family Four: a scaffolding-style frame and a 'pendular swing arm'!

out to be temperamental and required modification. In 1923 the Seal reached its final stage of development with two-seater Sport and Taxi bodies, and a Family Four with a narrow rear bench seat able to take two children. There was a return to chain transmission and the standard gearbox without a reverse. The Seal was produced in strictly limited quantities until 1928 when the manufacturer confined itself to its Progress utility models with their layout in the classic centre-front-wheel tricycle arrangement.

There were plans for an even more novel front-wheel-drive prototype, the New Progress, to follow the Seal in 1932, but the economic crisis, perhaps fortunately, nipped it in the bud.

The 1924 Family Four

The version described in detail here, the 1924 Family Four, is the only known surviving Seal and is on show at the National Motorcycle Museum in Birmingham.

Beginning with the cycle parts common to the whole unit: a chassis with parallel tubes held together with stirrup bolts, in the manner of scaffolding, rather than being brazed. According to Seal 'This method is superior in strength and flexibility to tubes weakened by brazing. As everyone knows, frame breakages always occur at the weakest spots, namely the brazing points.' The sidecar's body was supported at the rear on transverse leaf springs and the motorbike part – or what there was of it – lay between two rows of tubes. This simple arrangement became more complicated at the front, with a very curious pendular fork. The steering head pivoted at the top in a fixed double cradle; a swing arm comprising of two straight parallel tubes, fixed to the bottom of the steering head and pivoting on the lower part of the frame, rested on a large spring. A further novelty was the steering consisting of a single lever fixed behind the wheel on the steering column and linked by an articulated rod to the bottom of the front mudguard. With such direct control, it needed only a quarter turn of the wheel to the right or left to come up against the stops. The bike's rear drum brake and the sidecar's brake were foot operated (there was no front brake), but there was also an outer band brake on the outside of the motorbike's rear drum, which was operated by hand. Finally, while the throttle control, manual oil pump, electrics and spark advance controls were in the sidecar, the gear lever and hand brake remained on the motorbike, along with the starting pedal.

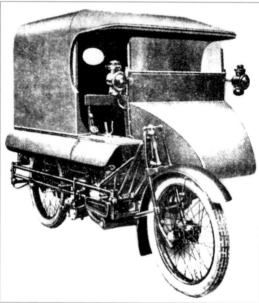

A Seal-Taxi about 1924.

● ● ● ● JAP two-cylinder, air-cooled V engine – 976cc (86.5 x 85mm) – 8hp – Dead end cylinders – Side valves – Total loss lubrication – Burman three-speed gearbox, lever operated – Single tubed frame for the motorbike and sidecar – Wheel and rod steering – Articulated front fork – Interchangeable wheels – 342kg unladen.

A first-generation Seal. The fork is a standard Druid and the frame much simpler.

Attaching a sidecar to a motorcycle is not a particularly great idea: all the weight is on the motorcycle side and when the sidecar is empty, it has a tendency to lift when the bike turns away from it. Then along came the Swiss logic.

MOTORSPORT SIDE-MOTOR (1923–1925)
A Swiss solution

The prototype bike and auxiliary sidecar with the engine of 1917.
(Museum of the Automatic Lathe, Moutier, Switzerland)

André Bechler himself poses on his strange motorcycle without an engine. (Museum of the Automatic Lathe, Moutier, Switzerland)

Five up on a Side-Motor! Might André Bechler have invented the perfect family vehicle? (Museum of the Automatic Lathe, Moutier, Switzerland)

A remarkable-looking motorcycle, but might there not be something missing?

The Side-Motor is one of the oddest attempts to restore balance to the sidecar by moving the engine into it.

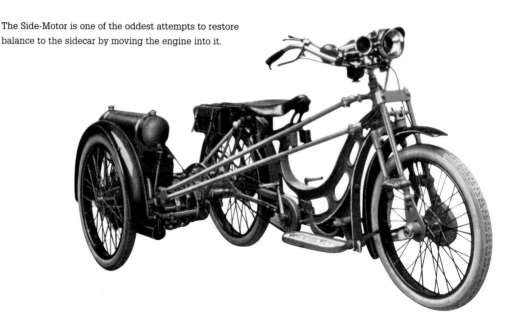

When he filed his first Side-Motor patent in 1917, André Bechler probably was not so much aiming to improve the sidecar's balance, but rather to make a unit as economically as possible. The 1917 prototype was in fact just an open-framed bike attached to a light tubular sidecar chassis supporting an engine linked to the bicycle wheel via two chains with an intermediate shaft.

From the watchmaker's lathe to the three-wheeler

Far from being a third-rate handyman, André Bechler was an outstanding mechanical engineer and businessman. A specialist in the Moutier clock-making industry, well known for its automatic lathes and headstocks, André Bechler established his first workshops in 1904 and his company, taken over by Tornos in 1974, remains to this day a world leader in the manufacture of automatic lathes. In parallel with his clock-making activities, Bechler also liked to express his love of all things mechanical through his second passion, motor vehicles. His creation of the Motosport company in 1923 gave him the excuse to indulge this passion, giving rise (among other projects including an interesting small car that was built between 1923 and 1925 but never put on sale) to the final version of the Side-Motor, which was essentially a proper motorbike with a side car attached... well, almost, since the engine was actually in the sidecar!

A certain logic

The principal idea of the Side-Motor was to put the engine and its auxiliaries in the sidecar rather than the bike, so as to create a better weight distribution. The engine, an excellent V-twin MAG made by Motosacoche of Geneva lay alongside the bike's rear wheel, a unique arrangement. A primary chain

linked it to the transverse gearbox that incorporated a clutch and two lever-operated speeds, and directly drove the motorbike's wheel. This was the sole powered wheel, but the sidecar's wheel was set on the same axis (contrary to the usual arrangement where the sidecar's wheel is placed further forward). As usual, the fuel tank was placed above the engine and perched above it was an uncomfortable-looking passenger seat.

A motorcycle without an engine would already have been a novelty, but André Bechler went even further, constructing an open-cradle motorcycle frame in cast metal, and adding a parallelogram front suspension that was unusual to say the least, with springs enclosed within the front fork tubes, inside which slid a central upper support attached to the steering head.

'A stable three-wheeler for the price of a motorcycle', claimed the Motosport catalogue, but Swiss customers, doubtless bound by tradition, were not convinced and sales were limited. However, the idea was by no means lacking in sense, and some 50 years later the engines in competition bike-and-sidecar units were working their way over towards the sidecar. The most obvious example was the revolutionary BEO, with its two driven wheels, built in 1978 by Beat Schmid and Guido Sieber (Swiss again!) and driven by Rolf Biland, whose engine was placed centrally between the two rear wheels.

Moutier now has a museum devoted to the history of the automatic lathe, where the amazing Side-Motor is displayed. (Musée du Tour Automatique: museedutour@bluewin.ch).

Strange, yet strangely logical.

After complex watches, the Swiss watch-making industry came up with the complex motorbike and sidecar!

●●●● MAG twin-cylinder, air-cooled V engine arranged longitudinally below the passenger seat in the sidecar – 495cc (64 x 77mm) – 4hp – Two speeds – Chain primary transmission and secondary via gears directly to the rear wheel of the motorbike – Pedal starting – Motorbike frame: cast, open frame – Parallelogram-fork front suspension – Sidecar chassis made from a triangular arrangement of straight steel tubes bolted together – 150kg – 50km/h.

'The stability of a three-wheeler at the cost of a motorcycle' claimed the 1923 catalogue.

The Side-Motor's curious parallelogram suspension.

The Side-Motor is no less striking viewed from behind.

Paradoxically, the three-wheeler has always been a part of the history of the motorised two-wheeler, from the early De Dion three-wheeler to more recent Harley-Davidson tri-cars used by the American police, as well as the still quite common Piaggio Ape. However, the tricycle with two front wheels is much less frequently seen.

THE SIDECAR LEADS THE WAY (1896-1934)
From Léon Bollée to the Tri-Moto-Berts

The famous Léon Bollée tricycle built between 1896 and 1900. At this time, the roads were clearly very stony.

The 1929 Tri-Moto-Bert, recently exhibited at Rétromobile.

There have been any number of three-wheeled delivery bikes, but very few types where the passenger sits between the two front wheels, ahead of the driver. Following Léon Bollée's 1896 steam tandem mini-car, there were a few imitators up until about 1908, usually as additions made from kits and attached to the front of the motorbike. Used by families, or even for racing, these 'tri-cars' such as Bruneau and Mototri Contal gradually disappeared in favour of the more user-friendly sidecar.

A revival of the obsolete

The early touring and sporting use of three-wheelers had died out by the late 1920s and the Blottos, Gallands, Juérys and Ninons that were left were purely delivery vehicles. Monet-Goyon, however, had specialised in three-wheelers for disabled people since it was founded in 1917. Was it looking for a way to increase its customer base? Whatever the case, the Mâcon manufacturer, who had already race tested a tri-car with the passenger seated ahead of the driver in 1922 and even marketed it as the VT3 Paris-Nice and the Cyclecarette, was clearly taken with the creations of Fernand Bert, their agent in Romans-sur-Isère. He had relaunched the idea in 1928, patented it and exhibited it at the October 1929 Paris Show.

Detail of the front assembly on a 1929 Tri-Moto-Bert. The engine has forced-air cooling.

Utility, touring and sporting vehicles

Much more refined than anything seen up until then, the Tri-Moto-Bert was distinguished by a suspended front chassis with a car-style steered leading axle, carrying either a goods body with a maximum payload of 300kg, or a sidecar body for sport or touring. All this was mounted in place of the front fork of a (preferably Monet-Goyon) motorbike.

The Tri-Moto-Bert was undeniably successful with more than 300 orders in the first year and with sales continuing into the late 1930s. Without any scruples, the Mâcon firm appropriated the idea at the same October show of 1929, where it exhibited its own Tri-Monet, very similar to the Tri-Moto-Bert. The rather cruder chassis was made from pressed steel, but it, too, had the car-type steering. The front part was detachable and one of the company's representatives was able to complete the process in 'less than half an hour'. The engine needed to be of a certain capacity and Monet-Goyon recommended either its Villiers 250/350cc engines, or its Swiss, four-stroke 350/500cc MAG engines with overhead or opposed valves. The Tri-Monet could be fitted with a standard delivery body or, in the de luxe version, a Bufflier sidecar from Lyon-Villeurbanne.

The tri-car concept with the passenger sitting at the front was to remain something of a side story, crowded out by the popular cyclecars of the 1930s, lightweight three-wheelers that offered an effective and economical alternative to the car.

An unusual meeting of three Tri-Moto-Berts in August 1932 on the Gap road over the Col Bayard (1,250m).

● ● ● ● Front chassis from tubes – Leaf-spring suspension – Fixed axle with pivoting stub axles – Steering by strut and track rod – Brakes on all three wheels, hand-brake on front, foot-brake at rear – Stabiliser to reduce rocking motion – Whole unit attached to steering tube and by spars at the footrests – Load 150 to 300kg as required, on utility version.

The most luxurious version of the Tri-Monet with an aluminium Bufflier Supersport body and the fine MAG engine from the Supersport 500.

The La Mure road at Mens.

Family outing on a MAG-engined Tri-Moto-Bert in 1934.

A stop on the Pont Neuf across the Isère at Romans.

A break on the road that snakes
through the La Mure Gorges.

Posing on the road from the Col de la Croix Haute
to the Col de Grimone... a climb of 12–14%.

A Tri-Moto-Bert based around a Monet-Goyon two-stroke Villiers. The Monet-Goyon-distributed models were enhanced by the addition of a cooling fan.

A 1929 advertisement from the Palais de la Moto, Grenoble.
The Tri-Moto-Bert's tubular front chassis is clearly inspired by the car.

Piaggio currently has a very successful articulated, three-wheeled scooter, the MP3. It's an open secret that nearly all the manufacturers are working on this kind of vehicle, which allies compactness and stability.

The Piaggio MP3 is actually no wider than a motorbike, while offering much better grip under braking (with two front wheels) and the same ease of driving, or rather, the same complexity since just like a two-wheeler, you can turn using the handlebars at low speeds, but have to rely on leaning into the bend at higher speeds.

At first sight, everything appears simple, and while no true articulated three-wheeler (two at the front or two at the rear) has ever been on sale before the Piaggio MP3, the articulated sidecar has had its moments in the sun.

It appeared in the mid-1910s both in Britain with Montgomery and especially in the United States with the 'Flxibles' that made Harley-Davidson so famous on cinder tracks. The idea of an articulated sidecar, sometimes with a wheel that the passenger could use to control its inclination, was later very popular in grass-track racing. On the track, Krause was a particularly noted specialist in Germany, while in France in 1937, Gnome & Rhône's dealer showed off its 'rocking' sidecar attached to a Gnome & Rhône CV2 500. Jeanneret offered it with a racing, sport or even a touring body with a hood and a windscreen, and to demonstrate the merits of its product, made brilliant use of it on local race tracks, in the 1938 Paris–Nice and the Geneva Grand Prix (winning it in 1937).

Some 34 years later, in 1971, another Frenchman, Jean-Claude Perrin, resuscitated the idea and created the Side-Bike Toro, which could easily be fitted to the Yamaha XT 600 and TDM 850.

In fact, articulated sidecars changed everything. Even a beginner could instantly feel confident and the unit could be driven just like an ordinary motorbike. The only difference was that the bike itself was just a little more

ARTICULATED SIDECARS (1916–1959)
Tilting wheels

difficult to balance, but everything else was so straightforward that one could soon find oneself taking corners at unimaginable angles, better even than a bike on its own, whether in the dry or the wet... although here one did have to be careful: a sidecar losing and then suddenly regaining grip could be unforgiving.

Driving across a slope was not the slightest problem, with the bike and the sidecar remaining vertical. Sexé still seems quite puzzled.

The rear view clearly shows the very simple attachment, hinged in two places with a system of linkages forming a folding parallelogram.

On articulated sidecars for racing, seen here with Krauser in 1959, the folding parallelogram (fitted the other way round compared with the Jeanneret) incorporates a rack and wheel that the passenger can use to control the angle of tilt.

Among the pioneers of the articulated sidecar, the 1916 'Flxible' included a spring to return it to the vertical.

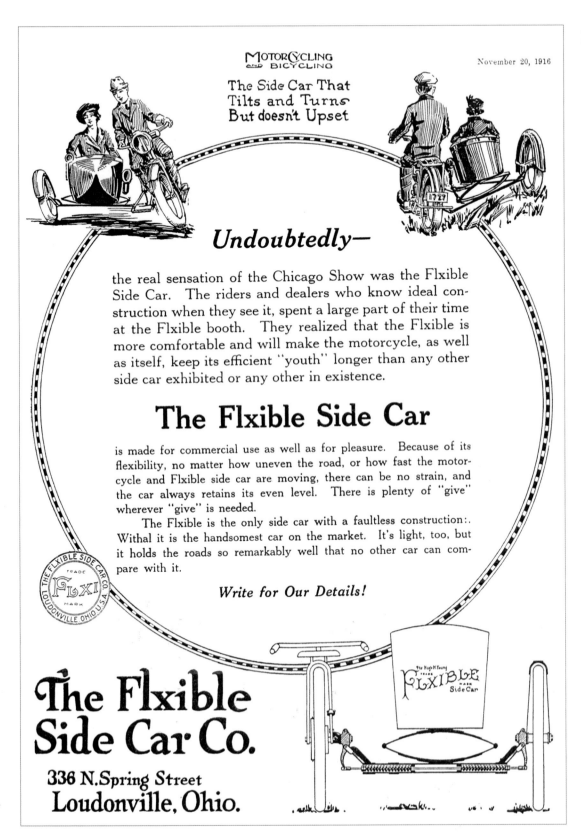

No problem taking a bend at 100kph claims this 1939 advert, and this has been verified. The problem is to regain control of the sidecar when it skids.

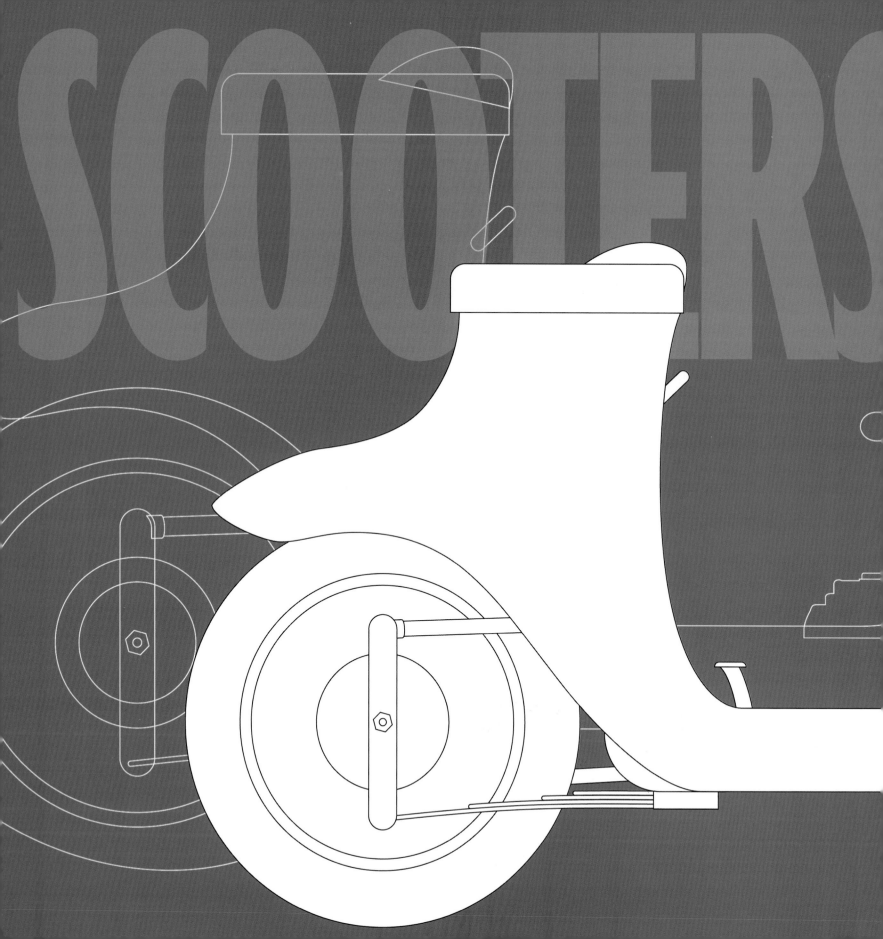

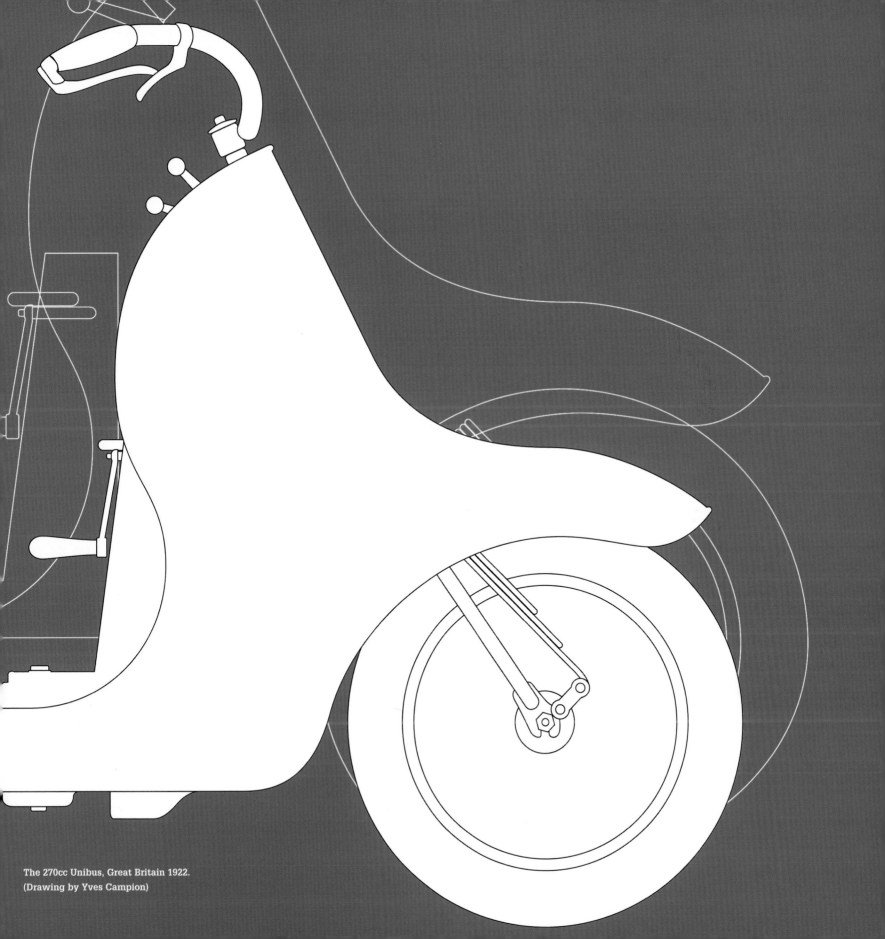

The 270cc Unibus, Great Britain 1922.
(Drawing by Yves Campion)

UNIBUS (1922) The first true scooter

This superb advertisement shows that the Unibus was aimed at a wide range of customers. What a pity it cost around £100, while a utility motorbike offering good protection, such as the Velocette EL3 Ladies Model with a three-speed gearbox could be bought for only £53.

It is tempting to see the ancestors of the motor scooter in the 1902 Autofauteuil or the Skootamota-style scooters of the early 1920s. However, the first true scooter to marry both the structure and the style inherent in this type of vehicle is the English Unibus of 1920, with its flat floor and wrap-around fairing.

The visionary Unibus was the product of the remarkable intuition of the chief engineer of the Gloucestershire Aircraft Company, Harold Boultbee, who was the first to create both the spirit and the form of the modern scooter. Unfortunately, it was 25 years too soon. As with almost every revolutionary product, it was a resounding commercial flop!

Still ahead today

Not only was it the prototype of the modern scooter concept, the Unibus is in some ways better than the scooter of today! The position of the engine at the front with a shaft transmission to the rear wheel ensured perfect weight distribution, while a proper 'bathtub' chassis consisting of two L-bars and welded metal triangles at front and rear would have given it exceptional rigidity. With front and rear suspension and a compartment under the seat, it really had everything, although we should perhaps not expect too much from the technology of the time. The swing front fork mounted on leaf springs probably wasn't all that effective and undoubtedly less so than the rear swing suspension also mounted on leaf springs in the manner of its contemporary and compatriot, ABC. Despite what you might imagine from the photos, the wheels were 16 inches in diameter, although they did carry very thin tyres. In another surprising modern touch, there were drum brakes both front and rear.

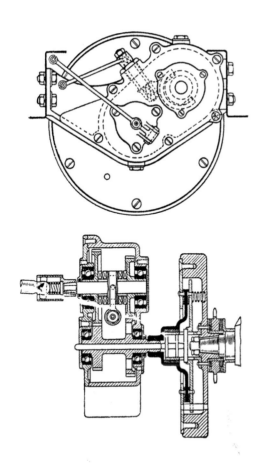

Side and overhead views of the gearbox.

The best was still to come

Revolutionary by any standards, the Unibus was much better thought out than the great majority of scooters turned out in subsequent years and even than many of those produced today, which may perform reasonably well, but are built on an unsound structure. Furthermore, the manufacturers had gone with 'reasonable' solutions because during the development stage they had tested a number of even more futuristic prototypes, including two with horizontal cylinders and silent-chain final transmission in an oil bath, and a third with an offset engine next to the rear wheel, a solution that Sir Harold Boultbee decided had no future!

A rare photo, taken in about 1922 in Copenhagen for an official display of the Unibus.

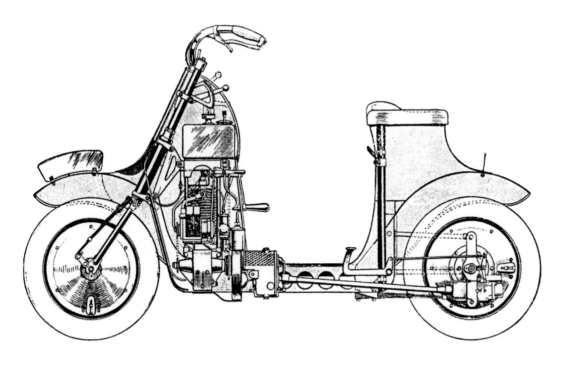

● ● ● ● Motor Precision two-stroke, single cylinder – 270cc (70 x 70mm) air-cooled – Separate gravity lubrication with drip feed – Two hand-lever-operated gears – Single-disc clutch – Starting handle – Shaft and worm-gear transmission – Chassis made from two steel spars with front and rear body in welded sheet – Bodywork: two pressed sheet-metal 'half-bodies' bolted to the front and rear of the chassis/floor pan – Pendular front fork with leaf springs, rear swingarm with leaf springs – Sheet-metal disc wheels with removable rims, 2.25 x 16in tyres – Drum brakes front and rear – 40km/h.

Like many factories that went over to building motorbikes after the war, the Gloucestershire Aircraft Company tried to do too much. This very clever, but also very expensive design sold in very small numbers between 1920 and 1922. Note the tube-mounted seat, which when swung sideways uncovers a small boot. Inside are the dry battery, the toolkit and a pump.

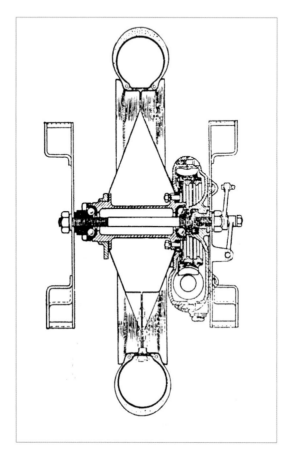

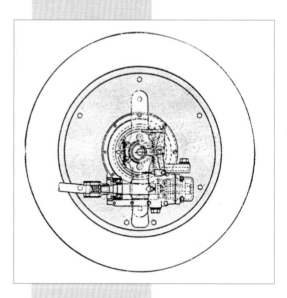

The rear wheel with its worm-shaft transmission.

The very car-like chassis consists of two steel girders holding a flat floor and front and rear sheet-metal supports to which the half-shells of the bodywork were bolted.

F ashionable in the early 1920s, both in Europe and the United States, the scooter was soon rejected because of its technical immaturity. After the Autoped, the scooterette of the 1910s, America regained its enthusiasm in the mid-1930s. Basic and playful, the Americans' new scooter was principally intended for use by families and students on campus. The feature that won them over was its simplicity.

SALSBURY
The inventor of the modern scooter

The Aero (1938): the first self-shifting transmission

The Salsbury Aero, still without a constant variable transmission (CVT) in 1937, but displaying a certain studied elegance.
(Herb Singe Collection; Dregni & Dregni)

There have been around 36 scooter brands across the Atlantic, more than 20 of which were in production between 1935 and 1946. Even Harley-Davidson tried its hand in 1959. For our purposes, let's forget the Cushmans, Crockers, Doodle Bugs, Moto Scoots and such. Many of them lacking bodywork and powered by lawnmower engines, these motorised scooterettes are of interest chiefly for their exoticism. One name does, however, stand out from the crowd: Salsbury, which was to invent firstly the automatic belt-and-pulley variator, then the Grand Touring scooter, the precursor of today's T-Max and Burgman. If history was permitted to retain only three scooters, there is not a shadow of doubt that they would be, in chronological order: the Unibus, the Salsbury and the Vespa.

Bing Crosby's girl trap
E. Foster Salsbury produced his Motor Glides in Los Angeles from 1936, even before Cushman, America's most famous scooter maker. Designed by Austin Elmore, they have the shape of a basic motorised scooterette, with tiny, five-inch wheels, no front bodywork, and a simple box at the rear topped with a cushion to cover the engine. Straightforward, but Salsbury took from this the five principles that he believed defined a scooter, and his definition remains relevant today:

The mounted police lose a bit of presence moving from the power of the horse to the 0.75hp of the 1938 Salsbury Motor Glide model 50, the first scooter with a CVT by variable pulleys. Only the policeman on the extreme right hasn't been allowed the De Luxe model with lights.

1. The engine is situated under the driver and usually just ahead of the rear wheel.
2. The frame is open and without any strengthening tube between the legs that obliges the driver to climb over it.
3. The engine is enclosed and fairings protect the driver's legs.
4. Small wheels, providing good manoeuvrability (instability, according to some).
5. Automatic transmission or a clutch and manual gear change.

A good businessman, E. Salsbury launched his Salsbury Motor Glide using the services of the most famous aviator of the day, Colonel Roscoe Turner, a holder of numerous records. 'The Salsbury Motor Glide is the biggest girl trap I've ever seen,' declared the colonel on the radio. The result was instantaneous: Bing Crosby (who really didn't need the help of such a trick) bought one, and the Motor Glide became the darling of Hollywood. The 1937 'De Luxe High Speed Motor Glide' was put into mass production and was even to equip police forces!

Boosted by this success, Salsbury introduced the Aero a month later, with its exquisite finish and a front mudguard styled in the shape of a water drop, a feature that was copied by all the other manufacturers. The typically Californian colours, bright red, or cream and jade were also a first. It was not until the 1950s that such stunning combinations would appear again, this time on cars.

Automatic in 1938!
Abandoning the two-stroke engine, the Aero was powered by a small 100cc Johnson engine with side valves. Offered in a number of versions, including one with a huge pizza-delivery-style rear boot, a sidecar model and one with two stabilising wheels at the rear for children, the Aero was much talked about but its sales were rather limited by American standards: 200–300 only.

There was a big change in late 1937: the new 50 and 60 models adopted the self-shifting transmission, a variator V-belt drive with double pulleys coupled to an automatic clutch. This inspired device, which today is fitted to every scooter, would be exported to Japan in 1948, where copies of the American system were used in the Fuji Rabbit.

As for Europe, apart from the 1957 DKW Manurhin, it was not until the 1980s and the invasion of Japanese scooters that the variator saw common use.

The height of fashion at the time, the very stylish little Salsbury appeared in many films. Actress Alexis Smith is seen here on a 1939 model 72. (Warner Bros)

Displayed with great pomp in Los Angeles in 1946, this is the De Luxe version of the Salsbury type 85.

B y the end of the war, the American mini-scooter had had its day, replaced by models that were equally basic, but much more opulent looking. The big change came once more from Salsbury, where the engineer Lewis Thostenson designed a much more refined engine, the precursor of all the big GT scooters of today.

At 2.28m long, the '85' launched with great pomp in Los Angeles in 1946 was blessed with aerodynamic lines whose substantial rear hid a spare wheel and a decent 40-litre parcels space. The front suspension was very much inspired by aeronautics, into which Salsbury was steadily moving. The telescopic component with two springs of different rating was incorporated inside the very long steering head, and a single tube held the wheel. At the rear, a single arm was supported on a single spring; the in-house engine was mounted on Silentbloc rubbers.

In line with the scooter's defining philosophy, the 85 offered maximum ease of driving: nothing on the handlebars, just two pedals that were not even described as 'brake' and 'accelerator' in the manual, but rather 'stop' and 'go'. There was a single drum brake on the rear wheel, as was normal at the time in the United States.

The 85 was available in two versions, the Standard, with an unusual body styling enclosing the front wheel and ending in a point under the handlebars, and the De Luxe with a wrap-around style and a large windshield (as well as an optional throttle!). But it had arrived too late on an American market where elaboration was not a problem and second-hand cars were increasingly affordable. Only 700,000 85s were built up until 1949.

The type 85 (1946) A GT maxi-scooter already

Reverse evolution

In Europe as in Japan many manufacturers had started in aviation and then turned to motorbikes after the conflict. Unsurprisingly, orders for fighters and bombers had dried up after the war, while people had a desperate need for a cheap means of transport. Salsbury, ever unconventional, followed the opposite pattern and went from scooters to... aeroplanes, being taken over by Northrop in 1947. Scooter production was transferred to Pomona, still in California, but the factory soon abandoned production of two-wheelers in favour of a curious precursor of the stealth bomber, produced by Jack Northrop between 1940 and 1949.

The Salsbury 85 De Luxe appeared in the catalogues with a sidecar, but did it ever go on sale?

Despite its impressive length, the Salsbury looked neat and much more elegant and slender than other big scooters like the 1965 Honda Juno or the huge Maicomobile. Note the passenger cushion and, in front of the seat, the handle that acted as a kick-start. (Scooter e Lambretta Museum, Rodano)

●●●● Four-stroke, single-cylinder, forced-air cooled – 318cc – 6hp at 2680rpm – Side valves – Automatic belt variator and clutch – Hand-lever starting – Chain final transmission – Frame from sheet-metal spars – Telescopic single-leg front suspension, single swing arm at rear – Single rear drum brake – 3.50 x 10in tyres – 140kg – 105km/h (65mph).

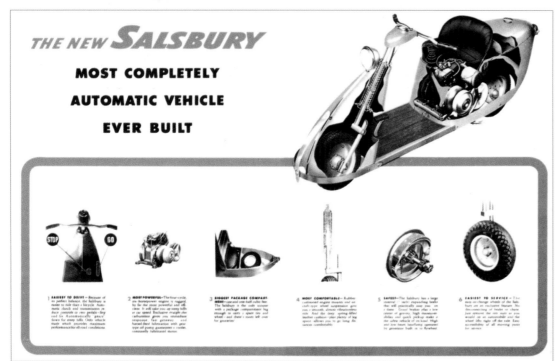

Despite what the driver's elegant outfit might suggest, this is just the Standard version of the Salsbury 85, lacking the big fairing. (Dregni & Dregni)

The catalogue highlighted the hi-tech features made use of on the Salsbury 85: single-leg front fork, automatic belt converter with just two simple positions: 'stop' for slowing down and 'go' for accelerating.

In the immediate post-war period, the German school of scooter manufacture quickly turned to ever bigger and more sophisticated models. Thus manufacturers and customers alike soon made the transition to cars. Nonetheless, BMW, the champion of distinctive, reliable and comfortable motorcycles, was tempted more than once by the scooter.

BMW (1947-1955)
False scooters and false starts

The idea of a small, utility BMW actually arose in 1947 with a very odd prototype known as the R10 (like the scooter that followed eight years later!). On this occasion, however, it was more of a motorbike, had it not been for the compact engine placed right up against the rear wheel, leaving an empty space ahead of it. Two prototypes were built, one of which was fitted with leg guards up to the height of the fuel tank, before the cost of producing such a sophisticated, but small-capacity machine signed the project's death warrant. Disregard the fuel tank and imagine the bike with slightly smaller wheels than the 16 inches it carried, and it is as if BMW had almost invented the first two-cylinder scooter, two years before the Italian Iso scooter and the British LE Velocette... And what a machine: a 125cc, two-stroke, transverse flat twin with rotary valve inlet. Created by the engineer Alfred Bönings, the design was inspired by Riedel's (the designer of the Imme) 270cc engine used as a starter motor for one of the first jet aircraft, the 1941 BMW 003.

First attempts

The first true scooter prototype appeared in 1953. Using the single-cylinder R25 as a starting point, it was a hybrid, part-scooter part motorbike, with large 16-inch wheels. The pre-production model had been readied and it was not until the last moment that the factory withdrew from exhibiting it at the October 1953 Cologne Show.

However, the idea of producing a scooter was not abandoned and in 1955 design work started on a new project, the R10. This time, the wheel diameter was the standard-for-the-time 10 inches, and the bodywork, which

The prototype R10 of 1947. Note the telescopic suspension with a single spring between the two legs of the fork. The box beneath the tank contains the battery and the toolkit.

was quite stylish compared with some other German scooters, was all flowing lines around the flat floor. Once again, the four-stroke, single-cylinder, pushrod OHV engine from the R25 served as a basis, with forced-air cooling and the capacity raised to 200cc. It was associated with a three-speed gearbox, operated either by foot pedal or hand. Suspension at the front and rear was a single-leg version of the Earles fork, and the R10 could put out between 8 and 10hp, well within the standards of the time.

Kept in the secret factory collection, this BMW R10, the first post-war prototype, made its first public appearance at the Salon Rétromobile in 1992.

Most unconventional, the R10's engine is a two-stroke flat-twin with its three-speed gearbox above the engine casing, as well as the encased carburettor. The magneto is on the end of the crankshaft. The footrests are ahead of the cylinders.

Too late then too early

The R10 project never came to fruition and as it was now too late to take advantage of the golden age of the scooter, BMW successfully devoted all its resources to motorbikes, until 1990, when it began to develop an unusual and ambitious idea for a safe scooter. The first design study for the C1 was shown at the 1992 Cologne Show. It would be a further two years before the project was completed and the C1 did not appear in its final form until the 1997 Frankfurt Show, before going into production for barely three years,

from late 1999 until 2003. It was probably too far ahead of its time and insufficiently well thought out to appeal to such a broad customer base.

A false start in 1947, two stillborn models in the 1950s and a commercial flop early this century... The story of BMW scooters is not a glorious one, despite the fine technological innovations. But all is not lost: we are now entering the golden age of large-engine-capacity scooters and BMW, always looking to broaden its range, might yet surprise us.

Irritated by the Velocette LE encroaching on its territory, BMW made a first cautious design for a scooter in 1953, but you can tell their heart wasn't in it!

A modern scooter, the R10 has front and rear swingarm suspension, as well as a transmission shaft reduced to its simplest form. As can be seen from the photo, it was actually used.

Much better thought through, the 1955 R10 scooter (reusing the 1947 prototype's designation) was, so it is said, turned down by the management only a few days before the Salon. A pity!

September 1951: Patuelli, head of the Motobécane test department, tries out one of the first SC prototypes on the brand-new test tracks at Montlhéry.

MOTOBÉCANE SCC MOBYSCOOT 125 (1951-1954) Superb, but...

Encouraged by the huge success of its Mobylette, of which it was making 1,000 a day in 1951, Motobécane exhibited a superb, novel, four-stroke scooter at the October show... but it was far from being fully developed!

Like an unwanted child, the scooter was born despite the views of management's top three, Charles Benoît, Abel Bardin and Georges de Grenier Latour, who didn't even hide from the press that they didn't have much belief in the future of this new type of two-wheeler. This was fortunately not the view of Éric Jaulmes, the technical director, nor indeed of the company's concessionaires, who were jealous of the growing success of the Italian Vespas and Lambrettas.

What does the directors' opinion count for, anyway? Éric Jaulmes got the green light and with the engineer Ernst Drucker created one of the most refined scooters of its time. It was one of the only European four-stroke scooters, along with the French Scootavia and the Guiller, both with AMC engines. On a restricted budget, the first Motobécane SC 125 shown at the 1951 Salon was powered rather feebly by the side-valve 125cc engine borrowed from the D45 motorbike, fitted for the purpose with a cooling fan. At 5,300rpm, the 4.3hp produced struggled to move the SC's 95kg.

The SCC that changed everything

After this false start, Motobécane renamed its never-marketed SC the SCC (STC by Motoconfort) and provided it with its own 125cc pushrod engine. This was not, as might be supposed, a modified version of the 125 Z2C claiming to put out 8.5hp, but a specifically designed engine for the Mobyscoot, even if a tiny bit less powerful – although no factory figures were ever published – and allowing it easily to reach 80kph. What a pity! The engine designed for a motorcycle, but not for a scooter, involves a very complicated gear change linkage operated by the left-foot double pedal.

It was the Motobécane's frame that showed the greatest innovation, with a chassis consisting of a large-diameter tube that split into two sections ahead of the engine and

The first 1951 prototype SC with side valves, identifiable from its three circular ventilation holes in the bodyside. On display at the Salon for 155,000 francs plus another 3,900 for a passenger seat, it would never actually go on sale.

The final development of the SC at the beginning of 1952 (with rectangular ventilation holes this time), proudly being presented by Mrs Patuelli. It disappeared off the price lists in July 1952. (Patrick Barrabès Archive)

with the front part acting as the exhaust silencer. Two plates attached to the rear held the swingarm pivot and joined the cradle tubes to the scooter's light-alloy rear body. The single cast-aluminium swingarm also served as the chain casing and compressed a conical spring backed up by a friction damper. The adjustment of the chain tension was unusual: the swing arm's axle/axis was moved by two standard tie-rods/struts such as are generally found on the rear-wheel axle/axis. Motobécane had not skimped; everything seemed perfect on paper. The exhaust pipe hidden in the frame turned out to be a good idea that went wrong. Though a neat solution, and successfully employed on the early Bernardets and the Paris-Nice Speeds, it had been badly designed in this case. It retained condensation and corroded rapidly to the point where there was a danger of it splitting. Another significant problem was residual grains of sand in the bottom of the fuel tank from the moulding process used for the aluminium rear body.

After a delayed launch, the manufacturer attempted to improve things with a final version at the 1953 Paris show, before the Mobyscoot passed the baton in late 1954 to the two-stroke Moby SB and SBH with prices starting at 95,000 francs, cheaper than a D45 S at 105,000 francs, while a Mobyscoot cost 168,000 francs (before being reduced to 153,000 in 1954). The benchmark Lambretta SD was 159,000 francs. Without shouting about it from the rooftops, Motobécane, fearing frame breakages that would have seriously damaged its reputation, discreetly tried to buy up as many of the Mobyscoots in circulation as it could. For this reason, the Mobyscoot is a rare and much sought-after item, especially as it made up for its youthful faults with a particularly attractive appearance, with a bit of Vespa at the rear and Lambretta at the front, while retaining its own character. This tour de force was down to the talent of artist Géo Ham (true name: Georges Hamel), who had collaborated with Motobécane since the 1930s.

With the side casing removed, you can see the SCC's hybrid design. The lower cradles are welded to a plate, which itself is bolted to the upper body and carries the swingarm's pivot and its tensioner.

Tilted slightly backwards, the engine, with a wide baseplate forming an oil reservoir, was purpose made. Note the complexity of the gear selector! (RTM Archive)

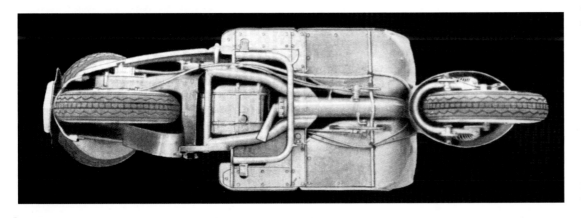

This view of the underside, taken from the excellent *Revue Technique Motocycliste* in 1953, shows the single-tube frame/exhaust pipe dividing under the engine and ending at the two plates that carry the single swing arm.

Above: The Motoconfort STC scooter (Motobécane's SC), seen here in its 1953 version, was not lacking in style and personality. (Didier Leclercq Collection)

Above right: A final version of the Mobyscoot appeared at the October 1953 Salon, distinguished by the almost rectangular shape of the side ventilation grilles. Sadly, it appears that Motobécane had sold its stocks of the previous version up to 1954 and this version was never put on sale.

Éric Jaulmes in the middle of a test run in late 1952, on the Col de l'Iseran 'road', which was still closed to traffic. It was tested alongside a pushrod SCC 125 and a Vespa.

To join the market after Vespa and Lambretta wasn't easy. But the stylist Géo Ham pulled it off.

'FLAT ONE' SCOOTERS (1951—1957)

A single horizontal transverse cylinder

The Ducati Cruiser of 1953: a real technological revolution.
(Didier Ganneau)

've always been attracted by the rare birds such as back-to-front engines and oddball transmissions. Going beyond the search for new answers, some engineers have set themselves the challenge of ignoring the accepted engineering methods and sought out the more unusual solutions. The 'flat one', in other words an engine with a single horizontal cylinder arranged transversally, is a perfect example.

This asymmetric construction provides a decisive advantage for scooters, where the motion of the suspended engine-transmission unit uses a lot of space under the bodywork. However, only three manufacturers have tried it, though they are by no means insignificant ones: Ducati in 1951, BSA in 1955 and NSU in 1957. As far as motorbikes are concerned, and for quite different reasons, this arrangement with the crankshaft on one side and the flat cylinders on the other would be taken up by BMW in its three-cylinder K 750 and four-cylinder K 1,000.

1951 Ducati Cruiser: simply too much

First out of the blocks was Ducati who caused a stir at the 1952 Milan Show with its Cruiser, a scooter with a four-stroke, pushrod OHV engine, hydraulic-converter automatic transmission and centrifugal clutch. Until then an electrical-industry specialist, the manufacturer came to making two-wheelers only a short time earlier with its Cucciolo moped. This time, the machine designed by the engineer Giovanni Fiorio and styled by Ghia was truly novel. However, this refinement and the cost it entailed would have a negative effect. The Cruiser cost half as much again as the contemporary Vespa and Lambretta, and only 2,000 were built between 1952 and 1953. Unlike in the later NSU with the

same cylinder arrangement, the engine was suspended and rigidly fixed to the frame. Only the transmission was incorporated in the swingarm (as on today's Honda Silver Wing). Bang up to date, the converter was locked automatically above a certain speed to prevent the slipping that this type of transmission was prone to, a device that has only recently been adopted in cars. It was sumptuously equipped: electric starter, side-mounted spare wheel (before Vespa!), hydraulic dampers etc. Sadly, the Cruiser was obliged to reduce its power output from 12 to 8hp so as not to exceed the 80kph speed limit then in force in Italy. Might Piaggio have been doing some lobbying behind the scenes?

1955: BSA Beeza

BSA did not do things by halves and entered the scooter market at the 1955 shows with two entirely novel machines: the 70cc, two-stroke Dandy, and the four-stroke, 200cc Beeza. To achieve maximum compactness, BSA not only arranged the Beeza's cylinder cross-wise on the left side, but also opted for side-valve distribution. Setting the valves at an angle of 45° allowed a rational layout of the combustion chamber, and the alignment of the crankshaft, four-speed, foot-operated gearbox and the shaft final transmission further helped with this objective. The cycle parts were just as original, with a tubed frame on which a

The Cruiser's mechanical side: a weighty unit, but highly compact. (Didier Ganneau)

suspended engine/transmission unit was mounted, and interchangeable, 12-inch wheels. But it was too good to be true, performance was poor and production would have been too expensive. It didn't last beyond the duration of the shows.

1957: NSU 'Teutonises' the Lambretta

NSU had been making Lambrettas under licence at Neckarsulm since 1950 under a five-year contract. At the end of the period, the contract was not renewed and in 1955, NSU brought out the Prima. The first version was powered by a 'made in Germany' development of the Lambretta engine with a vertical cylinder and shaft transmission. The

truly new version came along in 1957 (and sold up until 1960) with the Prima V, which exhibited all of the firm's technical know-how. One surprise was the 175cc engine, which remained a two-stroke (a four-stroke version would not get beyond the prototype stage), developed 9.5hp and followed the horizontal and transverse cylinder layout pioneered by Ducati. Very clever! A lot of space was thus saved and the crankshaft was in line with the gearbox (four speeds, pedal operated) mounted on the swingarm and driving directly on to the rear wheel via bevel gears. The Prima was further distinguished by its suspension, with particularly effective hydraulic dampers, an electric starter and... a 'Teutonic' style with a front mudguard resembling the shape of a Wehrmacht helmet. It's hard to shake off the past!

IL GRUPPO MOTOPROPULSORE DEL **DUCATI CRUISER**

Motore: monocilindrico orizzontale a 4 tempi.
Cilindrata: 175 cm³.
Camera di combustione: semisferica con valvole a V, comandate da un albero di distribuzione, posto nel basamento, a mezzo di aste e bilancieri.
Lubrificazione: a pressione sia per il manovellismo che per le scatole bilancieri, con pompa di ricupero.
Anticipo accensione: totalmente automatico.
Potenza: oltre 7,5 HP.
Velocità: 80 Km. h.
Consumo benzina: 3 litri circa per 100 Km.

Only the back end of the Cruiser, with its hydraulic converter and the transmission, is suspended.

The 1959 NSU Prima V really no longer owes anything to Lambretta. It weighs 138kg and can reach 90kph, excellent performance for the time. (Alain Urlings Collection)

A particularly full range of equipment.

The NSU Prima V: unlike the Ducati, the whole engine-transmission unit is suspended.

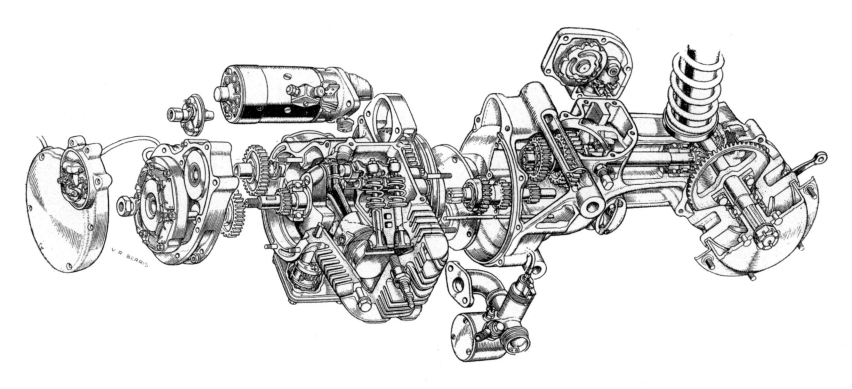

Had it been produced, the BSA Beeza would have been one of the last four-strokes with side valves. (Drawing by V. R. Berris – *The Motor Cycle*)

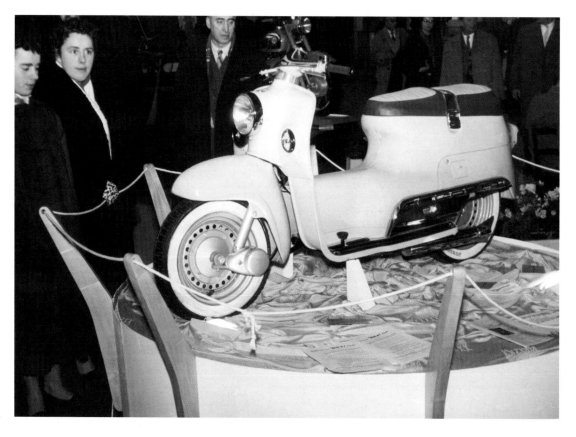

Perfectly logical, but much too expensive, the BSA 200cc Beeza.

These days there are practically no scooters with metal bodywork, either in steel or aluminium, but who were the first to try out plastic bodywork?

Being the first to design something is not easy, as months often pass between the announcement, the showing of a prototype, which may or may not be functional, and commercialisation... if it ever happens! It appears that the first scooter with plastic bodywork, or more exactly GRP (for glass-reinforced polyester), was the British Oscar, built in Blackburn by Projects and Developments and exhibited at the London Show in December 1953. It was a curious-looking machine, offered with 125cc or 250cc Villiers engines and an entirely British style of bodywork with an enormous double nose for which there seemed to be no real reason. Perhaps so that it looked like a car! The three-speed gearbox was operated by two pedals, the front and rear suspension was mounted on rubber blocks, the wheels had 12-inch tyres and the coupled braking was foot operated.

The use of fibreglass reinforced polyester was all the rage in Britain, where this new material was widely used on several scooters and later on streamlined motorbikes. The first firm to follow suit was Harper with its 1954 Scootamobile. Once again, Villiers engines (with a choice of two capacities) and a big nose were *de rigueur*, this time with a double headlight, an ample windshield and, still a rare luxury, an electric starter. In its 138cc form, the Villiers's 4.5hp was supposed to take the scooter's 105kg up to 80km/h (50mph). Next, but still in England, were the Bond Model P of 1958 and 1960, and the 1964 Velocette Vogue motorbike.

The use of plastic in other European countries was more cautious. In Holland, the Disselhof plant showed a prototype in 1956 that, aesthetically speaking, wedded the Mors front to the Vespa rear, with a 110 or 150cc engine and bodywork in GRP. It was not followed up, just as with the French Boudier Super B58 built by the aeronautical specialist Pierre Boudier and exhibited at the October 1957 Paris Salon. Powered by a standard 175cc Ydral engine, this stylish scooter was notable for its hydraulically controlled, coupled front and rear brakes. It had a single-tube frame and the plastic bodywork included a removable upper front section (removed in the photo).

PLASTIC SCOOTERS

Oscar (1953) And the prize goes to the British

OSCAR

THE BRITISH DESIGNED AND BUILT "OSCAR" has

★ **Accommodation** for two persons on a comfortable dual seat, space for two parcels, rider and pillion well protected from weather and mud.

★ **Silence and Smoothness** with its remarkable... Achieved by an exclusive design of exhaust silencer, together with resilient rubber mounting of the entire engine, gearbox and exhaust system.

★ **Exceptional Stability and Safety** ensured by the use of large wheels and... mounted on both sides to supple rubber suspension units.

★ **Outstanding non-skid characteristics** built into the design by unique suspension and correctly proportioned braking between front and rear wheels.

★ **Both Road Wheels Interchangeable** and easily removed by a single bolt without disturbing either final drive chain or brakes. A cushion drive is provided.

★ **Beauty of Line,** Accessibility and is easily cleaned.

OSCAR SALES (ENGLAND) LTD., Stamford House, 2-4 Chiswick High Road, London, W.4
Telephone: Chiswick 7829 & 7849

First displayed at the London Show in December 1953, the Oscar is here shown in the spotlight at the Brussels Salon the same year. Novy's intention to import them, however, would be restricted to the printing of a brochure!

The Bond Minibike in its P3 version at the 1959 London Show.

And in Japan, again

For a first attempt, it could be considered a masterpiece, especially from the aesthetic point of view. In 1954, Honda brought out its first scooter, the Juno K, a very imposing four-stroke, 220cc, OHV, 9hp machine with an all-polyester body whose style would not have been out of place among the wildest American designs of the period. It was available in two versions with either a single eye-level windshield, or a larger one with an extended top piece that folded back to a horizontal position to form a kind of roof. All in all, it was not quite as big a machine as its dimensions suggest: 2.07m long with a wheelbase of 1.4m would be considered normal for large scooters these days, but the difference came from the wheels, which were only 5.00 x 9in. With a claimed empty weight of 160kg, the Juno K actually tipped the scales at 195kg, despite its strikingly thin polyester shell, and it could reach a speed of 75km/h (47mph).

Some 23 years later, in 1977, Yamaha introduced the little 50cc Passola, which was the first scooter with an ABS body, a material that is used on all the current 'plastic' scooters.

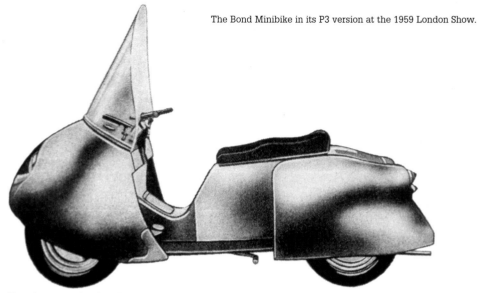

There's no question that the British sense of aesthetics is... well, different, as this dumpy 1954 Harper Scootamobile demonstrates.

Rather stylish, the Boudier Super B58, on show at the 1957 Paris Salon, is undoubtedly the first 'continental' plastic-bodied scooter.

Even more stylish is the Bond Minibike in its first P1 version of 1958.

The 1954 220cc Honda Juno reveals its innards with the rear body panels removed. (Scooter e Lambretta Museum, Rodano)

The Honda Juno is a match for any of the finest American designs of the 1950s. (Scooter e Lambretta Museum, Rodano)

The style of an era! The elegant lady showing off the Ondine in 1955 is none other than the wife of the managing director of Lucer, Jacqueline Degroote. (Georges Degroote Archive)

The 50cc Ondine with its 'plastic' body, a stylish product of the Lucer plant, appeared in France two years after the British Oscar. A late revolution? No, it was before its time. The manufacturing techniques were not fully developed and suspicious customers didn't turn up.

While not being the first motorised two-wheeler with polyester bodywork, the Ondine retains the privilege of being the first moped to use this material and, rarely among the pioneers of plastic, it was actually put into production, even if its sales were restricted to a few hundred in 1955 and 1956.

From planes to mopeds
Lucer (a small firm based in Hazebrouck, a town in the vicinity of Lille well known for its cycle industry) proudly announced its Ondine in August 1955 and showed it off in the Bagatelle Gardens and the Paris Salon as 'the first scooter-moped with a plastic body' (GRP). While the moped was certainly not without interest, the claim was nevertheless somewhat fallacious. It was unquestionably the first moped to use the material that had been created in the United States at the end of the Second World War for aeronautical purposes and which had appeared in some cars in the very early 1950s, but a number of other scooters had already made use of it, particularly in Britain.

The goddess of mopeds
Whatever the truth, Georges Degroote, the firm's owner, aided by his brother Roland, the construction manager, and Paul Duhamel, the workshop manager, had designed a very attractive little machine, whose initial sketches were allegedly made by the renowned designer Gedo. The various parts of its revolutionary bodywork were made by UCPA, normally a specialist in boat hulls, who had just opened a factory dedicated to polyester construction in the Paris region. The

Ondine (1955-1956) A bit too late or a bit too soon?

polyester cladding can be broken up into several sections: the rear shell, the front mudguard and a moulding incorporating the headlight, which was an extension of the seven-litre fuel tank. The engine, a German FTK Himo, allowed single-chain transmission as against two on the leaders in the field, Motobécane and Peugeot. Unfortunately, all this came at a price, and the Ondine went on sale at 69,500 francs at the 1955 Paris Salon, while the Mobylette ranged from 32,900 to 63,000 francs, and the Peugeot Bima from 38,000 to 49,500 francs. Despite the specialist press's enthusiastic reception, the poor little Ondine, insufficiently advertised and off-putting because of its advanced technology, lasted just one summer.

The Ondine is displayed at the Salon preview in the Bagatelle gardens. Georges Degroote, its designer, is in the middle and his brother Roland, on the right. (Georges Degroote Archive)